DATE DUE

BRODART   Cat. No. 23-221

Paying the
Social Debt

Paying the Social Debt

WHAT WHITE AMERICA OWES BLACK AMERICA

Richard F. America

PRAEGER

Westport, Connecticut
London

Library of Congress Cataloging-in-Publication Data

America, Richard F.
   Paying the social debt : what White America owes Black America /
Richard F. America.
     p. cm.
   Includes bibliographical references and index.
   ISBN 0-275-94450-6
   1. United States—Social policy—1980- 2. United States—Social
conditions—1980- 3. Income distribution—United States. 4. Social
conflict—United States.   I. Title.
HN59.2.A43   1993
305.8'96073—dc20   93-2861

British Library Cataloguing in Publication Data is available.

Library of Congress Catalog Card Number: 93-2861
ISBN: 0-275-94450-6

First published in 1993

Praeger Publishers, 88 Post Road West, Westport, CT 06881
An imprint of Greenwood Publishing Group, Inc.

Printed in the United States of America

∞™

The paper used in this book complies with the
Permanent Paper Standard issued by the National
Information Standards Organization (Z39.48–1984).

10 9 8 7 6 5 4 3 2 1

To My Great Grandparents,
William Anderson and Ellen Craighead Anderson,
Samuel Goode and Elizabeth Pitts Goode,
Francis Caldwell and Mary Millis Caldwell,
and
Moses America and Clara Price America,
whose generation, and those before, helped build the country, but went
largely unrewarded.
And to Robert F. Kennedy and Martin Luther King, Jr., who seemed
to intuitively understand that reparations are justified and will benefit
the nation many times over.

Fondly do we hope, fervently do we pray, that this mighty scourge of war may speedily pass away. Yet, if God wills that it continue, until *all the wealth piled by the bondsmen's two hundred and fifty years of unrequited toil* shall be sunk, and until every drop of blood drawn with the lash shall be paid by another drawn with the sword, as was said three thousand years ago, so still it must be said, "the judgments of the Lord are true and righteous altogether.

—Abraham Lincoln

Every idea is an incitement.

—Oliver Wendell Holmes, Jr.

Contents

Preface

We should pay the have nots, the poor and marginal, what we owe them. We can do that by investing in their education and training, housing, and health. That will benefit them and all the rest of us. We should also invest in crime prevention, business formation, and community development. That will help the poor and marginal become independent and fully functioning contributors to society. In the end, all this assistance will ease the financial and psychic burden on everyone else and will increase U.S. productivity and competition.

Our present economic distress can be traced in part to the economic injustices that the haves' ancestors committed against the have nots' ancestors. This indictment, though all inclusive, is essentially correct and conceptually helpful. Those injustices produced wrongful benefits that have been passed on to the present day, creating an imbalance that has damaged economic performance and caused social instability. The tax and budget system may be employed to remedy these imbalances. We should adopt specific, targeted, and time-limited income and wealth redistribution because it's right and because it's essential to our nation's current and future well-being. The unjust enrichments unbalance the economy, and these injustices alienate and demoralize millions who react by withholding their best efforts and by behaving in ways that in the end impose high social costs. That reaction undermines overall economic performance and diminishes the United States' competitiveness and productivity.

The book proceeds this way. First it shows one way to estimate the current value of some of the income diverted from have nots to haves. Then it deals with the reality that the idea of restitution usually is unpalatable, and encounters a negative first reaction, even from socially progressive people. Next, it outlines how to redistribute capital in ways that enhance overall economic performance. The way to make restitution is not through handouts and income transfers, either cash or in kind. Instead, the best way is through investments in education, health, housing, training, crime prevention and business development. These are capital transfers. They help the have nots contribute to the economy and become self-sufficient.

The book then introduces a theory of social monopoly as an antitrust concept. And it proposes subsidized corporate redistribution as another innovative way to make restitution. Then it examines poverty from the restitution point of view, shows how affirmative action should work and how it should be designed as a way to redistribute capital, and examines how crime, and self-destructive behavior by the poor and marginal, prevents local investment and job creation, and how increased investment in crime prevention will help pay the debt and boost the economy.

It examines how curing chronic dependency and family dysfunction will help pay the debt, and shows how to prevent crime and discourage much of those other kinds of destructive behavior, by putting new emphasis on persuasive communications that promote the idea of "behave yourself."

Finally, it examines the tax structure and offers ways to get tax reform by using restitution theory to correct injustices in the way we levy taxes, and applies restitution theory to the debate over how to become globally fully competitive and productive.

Acknowledgments

This book took shape over thirty years. The basic ideas began to form in Cambridge in the early 1960s. I thank Fred Wallace, Harry Denny, Conrad Harper, and John Hatch for many hours of extended, and sometimes raucous discussion on all aspects of the race question over the dinner table.

The specific concept formed in the tumultuous days of Berkeley and Palo Alto in the late 1960s. Over the years, I debated the possibility of reparations as a serious, constructive public policy tool, especially with Robert Browne and David Swinton.

Bob Arnold at Stanford Research Institute, Mike Winston at Howard University, Gerry Udinsky, and Bernadette Chachere, and Chuck Lucas, at U.C. Berkeley, all enriched my thinking.

Thanks to the San Francisco Foundation and the Rockefeller Foundation for indirect support. And thanks to the members of the National Economic Association, carrying on the battle to make sure pathbreaking economic and policy analyses, on issues of racial justice, continue to get a full hearing.

Dick Holton and Ed Epstein, at U.C. School of Business, and Gerald Bach at Stanford Business School, made administrative and teaching arrangements that created opportunities to develop this and other projects.

Thanks to James Dunton, Arlene Belzer, Denise Van Acker and Betty Pessagno at Praeger Publishers. Restitution is a controversial idea, one that many publishers would avoid or even actively oppose and seek to suppress. I'm grateful Praeger has seen fit to provide a forum in which a disturbing but potentially highly constructive and beneficial notion can find an audience and, perhaps, help bind up and heal the nation's wounds.

My wife, Dino, and daughter, Amy, let me work in the "cave" to my heart's content, and I thank them for the space and good wishes.

Introduction

. . . an imbalance between rich and poor is the oldest and most fatal ailment of republics.

—Plutarch

Injustice ruins civilizations.

—Ibn Khaldun

Something is wrong in our country. As we look back over the years since World War II, we see growth, progress, and success, and much that inspires pride. At the same time, too many signs are mixed and too many trends are down. For example, at one point in 1991, one out of ten Americans was on food stamps.[1] We are clearly in economic trouble, and getting back to robust health and staying there doesn't seem to be just around the corner, as so many would have us believe.

The period since the outbreak of the Vietnam War has been marked by economic and social troubles. This period witnessed higher total output, corporate equity, and real estate booms, but survey after survey reveals a peopled plagued by fear, insecurity, anger, and ambivalence. And we nervously pose the question: Are we on the right track?

All Americans—the haves, the middle classes, and the have nots alike—have been told that some unpleasant changes may be permanent and that the world may have changed in ways that will mean less for America. That would mean less for them. Those in the middle resent the idea that the haves did so well during the 1980s by using methods that seemed a bit unfair. They also don't like to see government attention and resources focused on the have nots. To the middle, both the haves and the have nots appear to have made out at their expense, and they want an end to that injustice.

In the 1990s the nation's political leaders will have to juggle conflicting demands and will need to explain several delicate realities. Creating and sustaining broad economic prosperity requires a wise and balanced tax program that is both equitable and efficient. Unfortunately, discussion of taxes has been distorted by the Reagan and Bush administrations. The "No New Taxes" pledge made by Bush in 1988 had an emotional appeal that helped him win the election, but it was an immensely mistaken and foolish pledge.

Fiscal discipline and budget control are essential, and the widespread waste in government must be eliminated. But in deciding what to do, too many leaders base their actions on the emotional response of volatile swing voters. So it is that income tax increases, capital gains cuts, property tax changes, and other tax shifts, all of which can create or destroy economic incentives, are formulated. In so doing, they affect the nation's productivity, creativity, and total output.

Proposals to adjust the tax structure are made continually. Whether the economy is expanding or contracting, ideological posturing never ends, and the clarity and understanding of basic issues is never fully attained. As is true of every policy, tax policy that will just please the majority is not desirable. Rather, policies that will also lift the have nots are a necessity. What is the fundamental rationale for this thesis?

Taxes affect overall efficiency and resource allocation, but they should also produce equity. They have a legitimate redistributive function. That is, tax policy should also compensate for inherent injustices in the market. No tax policy will strengthen the economy and truly benefit the middle classes until they acknowledge that taxes should, in part, raise revenues to make restitution and pay the social debt. The middle classes reject this message because they believe that as a result their gains will slip away. They show their rejection by revolting at the polls, punishing incumbent politicians, withholding taxes that would go to the have nots, and punishing the haves by withholding cooperation and commitment at work and through government. But in the end that behavior is self-defeating. So what to do?

The middle classes are preoccupied with the problems of waste, fraud, corruption, and greed; "them"—the Japanese, Germans, immigrants, and the have nots; coddling, permissiveness and social decay; and the loss of "family values." They have been led to believe that the answer is to get tough, but they have been misled. While all those factors play a part in creating the uncomfortable situation and all contain some truth, they do not in the end explain the problem. As a result, wrong remedies are applied, making matters worse.

The missing element in this explanation of the problem can be summarized this way. The haves have incurred a social debt for which they owe restitution. To get to the heart of the systemic problems that afflict most Americans, we need to step back and look at race, class, history, behavior, and justice. All the most widely discussed analyses of the last thirty years contribute insights. But they all miss a key final ingredient. That is why policy is confused, troubled by finger pointing, blame, hostility, mistrust, and fear of the future.

We have avoided the obvious problem. If we acknowledge it and deal with it accordingly, we—our children, and their children—will prosper.

RESTITUTION THEORY

Stated simply, **Restitution Owed = The Net Present Value of the Sum of Deviations from Fair Standards in Prices + Wages + Employment + Interest + All Other Transactions.**

Wherever there is chronic, protracted conflict between groups, nations, or races, invariably we find an underlying grievance over historic economic injustice. The grievance is not usually well understood, formulated, or articulated. Always, however, one party believes that it has been wronged and that the other party benefits from that injustice.

Historic economic relations can be reconstructed, and actual patterns of labor, trade, and investment relations can be audited, long after the fact. A set of "fair" wages, occupational distributions, employment levels, prices, interest rates, educational expenditures, taxes, profits, and returns on investment can be posited, and deviations from those "fair" standards can be estimated. The deviations, which will usually be found to have resulted in part from force, manipulation, and coercion, can be aggregated, compounded, and price adjusted. That will yield a "bill" that represents the monetary basis for the current conflict, which heretofore neither party realized. The bill can then be negotiated, and rational, feasible settlement agreements can be reached, thereby avoiding violent and other common dysfunctional responses.

ECONOMIC JUSTICE

This book focuses on the 1990s. While the proposals offered here are timely, the major theme is timeless. Economic injustice spans the entire history of the United States, and it will continue as long as groups try to dominate other groups economically.

The problem has been with us for centuries, hurting the nation all that time. Understanding the policy implications of restitution theory would have helped the Untied States avoid economic and social malfunctions throughout the twentieth century. It would also have been useful in expansive good times, because the seeds of future trouble are present even in times of prosperity. Applied consistently, restitution theory can help us avoid piling up future social debts and then having to repair the damage.

By taking better account of inequities, we can operate more efficiently. By ignoring them, we can be assured that the roller coaster of national life will be bumpier, more frightening, and far more costly than necessary.

THE PRIMARY SOCIAL DEBT

Whites owe blacks money, roughly several trillion dollars. Actually, only *some* whites owe blacks money; most do not. While most of the debt is owed to poor blacks, all blacks have been victimized by centuries of economic injustice in ways that benefit whites in the top 30 percent.

That constitutes the United States' primary social debt. Other groups may also deserve priority attention for similar reasons, but the debt that contributes most to national instability and dysfunction is white-to-black. Although this idea is intuitively obvious, it has not yet been accepted by the mainstream, primarily because it has not made the connection between chronic economic and social underperformance and the social debt.

Yale Law School's Boris Bittker clearly outlined much of the concept in 1972 in his important and path-breaking book, *The Case for Black Reparations*.[2] Few grasped its significance then, for the nation was still enjoying the postwar boom. Ironically, now that economic hardship has become more widespread, restitution theory may at last find a more receptive audience. Nonetheless, twenty years after Bittker, we are still spinning our wheels, and racial dialogue has become even more strident and polarized. By avoiding the real issue, many aspects of social performance and community life have worsened.

Is there a better way to state the basic conclusion that whites owe blacks money? Surely, a more diplomatic way to express the idea exists, but any other phrasing would simply fudge the message. In this book, the idea is couched in terms of relations between haves and have nots. Moreover, the problem is addressed in the context of what is good for the country and for its overall economic performance. At the same time, a bottom-line truth must be grasped. There is this debt. Until we get that straight, the intellectual and political logjams and bottlenecks on race and poverty will remain. That means basic economic policy will remain confused, out of focus, and unsuccessful.

THE SOCIAL DEBT

What is the social debt? It is the haves' unjust enrichment of several trillion dollars—$5 to $10 trillion—by some estimates, in the form of wealth, income, or expected lifetime earnings. It is the amount over and above what they would have earned, relative to what the have nots earned, in the absence of slavery and discrimination. It would rightfully have gone to the have nots had there not been systemic injustice.

Who are the haves? They include everyone, as a class, whose current or probable future income is in the top 30 percent of the income distribution—specifically those earning over $40,000 a year. They include those whose ancestors came through Ellis Island or other ports, as well as those whose ancestors came over on the *Mayflower*, or fought in the Revolution or the Civil War.

The have nots are those in the bottom 30 percent, those earning or receiving transfer payments under $15,000 a year. It disproportionately includes the focus of this book, African Americans. Thus, restitution theory and the concept of the social debt are about group benefits, losses, rights, wrongs, obligations, and entitlements.

This even flies in the face of the emerging attitude in some important quarters, including a majority of the Supreme Court. In the early 1990s, the Court tried to narrow the focus and to apply a strict constructionist interpretation, insisting on proof of individual damages and responsibilities in civil rights and affirmative action matters. Restitution theory directly rejects that approach.

RESTITUTION AND THE GENERAL WELFARE

There are two schools of thought on how to approach restitution. One is that the debt is indeed owed and should be paid. It is not couched in terms of the general welfare, and it is not concerned with understanding how paying it will enhance overall social well-being. This view simply argues that the moral obligation is unconditional and binding, and it takes no account of whether paying it would benefit everyone. The second view is a practical one. It acknowledges the existence of a debt but maintains that the concept will attract broad general support, and thus be paid, only if it is made clear that doing so is not only moral but also practical and broadly beneficial.

This book takes the second point of view, but it acknowledges the moral correctness of the first. Specifically, the argument presents some insights on the tangled problems of general economic inefficiency, global competitive disadvantage, urban decay, social disintegration, race relations, poverty, crime, and self-destructive behavior.

This discussion also deals with another kind of intangible social debt: namely, the have nots owe themselves and society a high level of performance that has been lacking in recent decades.

A PRACTICAL CONCEPT

In 1990 New York Mayor David Dinkins convened a special meeting of big city mayors to come up with a united urban agenda. It had been years since that kind of national policy had been urged. Two years later, in 1992, riots occurred in Los Angeles following a controversial jury decision involving four white police officers and a black motorist, who by chance had been videotaped while being beaten by the officers as he was taken into custody. There followed the widest and deepest discussion of race and economic justice in over twenty years.[3] The discussion was flawed, however, because it was based on the same assumptions as those that had informed the Kerner Commission that investigated the causes of the series of riots in 1968.

The early 1990s also witnessed a continuing flow of books on race and economic distress. All these books zeroed in on key elements of the problem and made valid points and useful recommendations. None was willing or able to come to a useful conclusion about the role of exploitation. None seemed to make the full connection between urban conditions, race relations, the United States' general competitiveness and performance concerns, and historic systemic injustice. If we are to effectively build sound policies in the 1990s so that we can enter the next century with confidence, we have to understand how economic justice figures in the equation.

SLAVERY AND DISCRIMINATION

How did the debt originate? First, there was slavery. It directly enriched those who bought, sold, transported, financed, bred, leased, and managed slaves in agriculture. But it was also important in other sectors, including mining, transportation, manufacturing, and public works—roads, dams, canals, levees, railroads, clearing land—and so on.[4]

It indirectly benefited millions who had no first-hand contact with slavery, affording them the benefits of slave-produced goods and services and releasing them from low-level occupations so they could pursue more rewarding life's work. It also freed them to receive education and training of greater value to them, and, as it turns out, to their descendants, than they would otherwise have had, absent slavery.

Second, the debt can be traced to discrimination, especially in education and employment. Most Americans disapprove of discrimination on the basis of its unfairness. But it does produce tangible benefits, most of which are realized indirectly and passively. That fact makes the subject tricky to explain and difficult for many to grasp.

Discrimination is good for someone, but most people have chosen to pretend to think of it as merely unkind or socially unfair. Restitution theory strips away the pretense. It lets us see how discrimination has indirectly enriched millions of people relative to those who have been excluded. The social debt, when acknowledged and paid, will help restore the have nots as a class to something approaching their rightful place.

To use the Supreme Court's language, an "amorphous" injustice is operating throughout the economy. Restitution theory can help clarify and remedy heretofore unrecognized wrongs. The trouble is, that this notion collides with some of our most deeply entrenched assumptions: that we have individually arrived at our place in society, fair and square; that equal individual opportunity has been secured for all; and that everyone can now go forward, unfettered by membership in any class, group, or race, to make it by adopting working/middle-class values. Thus, restitution theory contradicts long-standing assumptions and beliefs. It respects and shares the assumption of the utility of individual responsibility, but at the same time it asserts that group dynamics still account powerfully for personal well-being or misfortune, as the case might be.

THE SOCIAL DEBT AND NATIONAL COMPETITIVENESS

Some analysts contend that we should acknowledge the debt and pay restitution. But how does all that really affect the overall national ability to produce, grow, innovate, and maintain or improve our standard of living and our competitive position in a dynamic world economy? How is it relevant in those practical terms?

The answer is, millions of Americans are disenchanted, alienated, and underperforming. Many intuitively sense they are victims of a massive historic and ongoing injustice. Many also sense a connection between their situation, as a class and the haves' affluence and general relative good fortune. Their self-defeating and dysfunctional behavior costs them, as it does all of us, both directly and indirectly.

We should help upgrade the have nots' lives and performance both because it is the right thing to do and because it makes practical sense. If the have nots obey the law, stay healthy, get educated, and perform economically, social "safety net" costs, which are grossly and unnecessarily high, will be greatly reduced. The burden on budgets—municipal, county, state, and federal—will decline, and the have nots' output and enhanced capacity to earn, produce, consume, save, and invest will be felt throughout the entire economy at every level.

THE MORAL BIND

One key to understanding why such a debt should be recognized and paid is the moral dilemma. The haves want the have nots to stop committing crimes, destroying property, procreating irresponsibly, underperforming in general, and imposing the resulting financial, opportunity, and psychic costs on others. In other words, the haves want the have nots to shape up and act like working- and middle-class good citizens—to live by sound "family values." Simply put, they want them to behave themselves. But there's a bind. The haves find it difficult to take a consistent and firm stand, and insist on these behavioral standards because, privately, they know that they themselves are misbehaving. They sense that they have unclean hands, too. They intuitively know they have continued to accept and enjoy an unjust enrichment and recognize that it derives from past practices that are now considered to be wrong. They also sense that they are benefiting at the expense of the have nots. This situation cannot continue to go unremedied.

The have nots know all that, too, and they, too, recognize that the haves are in a moral bind. In essence, then, a game is being played. For both parties to escape their bind, they have to face up to the games they have been playing. A kind of national transactional analysis is needed to help them end the collusion in not mentioning the obvious. Sooner or later, everyone has to acknowledge this pattern and then change it. Only then will it be possible to hold everyone to normal standards of performance and self-discipline, expecting everyone to give a full contribution and a fair day's work for a fair day's pay.

How do slavery and past discrimination interfere with the have nots' ability to participate fully? This question is not an invitation to recite the culture of poverty theory. That concept states that self-destructive behavior is embedded in underclass settings, binding people, generation after generation, so that few can escape. Instead, restitution theory states that, over the centuries, the haves have deprived the haves nots of investment in their training and education. This pattern and practice has benefited the haves, producing compounded benefits for the haves' descendants but compounded loss of knowledge, skills, and abilities for the have nots' descendants. As a result, after 350 years of theft of human capital and education, the have nots cannot function in the modern world. The solution is to train and educate them to carry their share of the load. Their defects are dragging the whole economy. Instead of contributing at their appropriate level, they require support and subsistence subsidies, wealth that could be better spent to enhance the nation's overall performance.

PUT ALL THE CARDS ON THE TABLE

Further refinement and research will finally establish, once and for all, the size and full extent of the social debt. The goal of the present work, however, is far simpler. It seeks to make the basic case for restitution, offering illustrative technical analysis and examples of how the debt operates. It also proposes remedies. The social debt concept can help us find a better approach to chronic related problems of poverty, crime, racial conflict, and economic inefficiency and underperformance. The book will help us think about issues that constantly assault us in the headlines—riots, police brutality, family values, single parent–female-headed households, welfare abuse, affirmative action, minority business contract set-asides, crime, homelessness, teen pregnancy, crack babies, drugs, unemployment, ugly public housing and transportation, street people, panhandlers, traffic congestion, labor unrest, school dropouts, AIDs research, the balance of trade, the deficit, savings and loan bailouts, leveraged buyout and junk bond scandals, environmental degradation and pollution, bureaucratic waste, fraud, abuse, and mismanagement, corporate executive pay and perks, congressional reform, political action committee/lobbyist/special interest abuses, tax reform, voter apathy and cynicism, and so on. Restitution theory touches them all.

But we may wonder, "How is history our responsibility? Why can't we just assure everyone an equal full opportunity from now on? Why are we responsible for the sins of our fathers? The answer to the last question is that we are not accountable for our fathers' actions, but we are responsible for our own sins. One of those sins is accepting and keeping inherited benefits that were wrongfully produced in the first place, that were then wrongfully bequeathed to us as members of a large class, and that helped deprive other people of their rightful place. Most of us have never thought about race, poverty, and social conditions this way. However, we can at least understand that many people believe that history has an enormous impact on current affairs. Through this book we may also be able to discuss economic and social policy with a new awareness of why redistributive justice is so elusive and why it is so essential.

WHAT'S PAST IS PROLOGUE

Restitution theory is straightforward. From 1619 to the present, various forms of past discrimination have benefited large classes of haves, not just those who directly discriminated. Those classes then passed those benefits on to succeeding generations in their class, not just to their actual legal and biological direct descendants.

The debt can be paid in ways that are practical, fair, democratically debated and decided, and beneficial to the entire country. As with any new policy idea, however, we might ask, how can it be tested with the minimum risk of producing unanticipated and counterproductive consequences? This book presents one way we can think more constructively about the related problems of general economic inefficiency, race relations, poverty, crime, and self-destructive underclass behavior. Restitution theory gives a sound basis for practical action.

PUTTING JUSTICE FIRST

Once we recognize and remedy economic injustice for its own sake, we will also help strengthen the overall economy. Deep injustice pervades our society in the form of discrimination and exploitation based on gender, ethnicity, race, and religion. All these kinds of injustice should be discouraged and remedied. As one important example, we can look at racial discrimination and seek ways to approach the problem that will enhance economic performance. Restitution theory is not a matter of doctrine. Rather, it is an objective idea that practical liberals, conservatives, whites and blacks, Republicans and Democrats alike, can use to help manage the economy.

We need to recognize that chronic poverty diminishes economic output, imposes unnecessary costs, and is substantially rooted in past injustice. We should also recognize that past injustice against the have nots produces current benefits to the haves. That is a social debt and creates a need to make restitution. We can pay restitution by investing in housing, health, education, employment, training, crime prevention, affirmative action, and small business development.

LOSING GROUND? WHY?

Why does the United States seem to be losing ground relative to its key competitors? Why is the United States uncertain of its place as leader in global economic and industrial competition? There is no shortage of explanations. Some observers actually insist that these perceptions are faulty and that we really are not relatively worse off. But in truth we have retrogressed. We tolerate continuing economic injustice, and that erodes our spirit, strength, and energy. Until we remedy those wrongs, we will not be fit and fully healthy again, and able to continually generate jobs, meet domestic and international responsibilities, and provide income sufficient to enable all citizens to live in security and with peace of mind.

One seminal event in the late 1980s signaled the weakness of the U.S. economy: the partial collapse of the stock market in 1987, especially the 500 point drop on Blue Monday, October 19. Analysts groped to explain this cataclysmic financial event. Business and political leaders called for policy changes to strengthen the dollar, adjust trade balances, stimulate exports, slow imports, encourage savings, target investments, and cut deficits by tax and budgetary reform. Some analysts stated that we needed to retrain millions of people and offer incentives to upgrade productivity and general working behavior. That means we have to correct inequities, because behavior is influenced by feelings about fairness.

We must acknowledge and pay the social debt and progress toward broad systemic justice, for everyone's needs are involved. The have nots can obviously benefit from direct targeted programs. The middle class, the middle 40 percent, need reassurance about job security, health, housing, education, and secure retirement. And the haves, the top 30 percent, need creative opportunities, as well as an environment and climate that is conducive to successful investment. This investment can create jobs and new products and services that will be to everyone's benefit.

CORPORATE POLICY AND RESTITUTION

The business sector also needs to accept the restitution theory. Innovative managers in operating units, planning, financial, human resources, and marketing, as well as in public and government affairs, can use the concept creatively. Based on this theory, public affairs executives should be able to create new community relations, government relations, and philanthropic strategies, which will enhance their firms' reputations as progressive in their dealings with people and communities.

Sensitive issues involving race continue to hamstring most executives. Restitution theory will help clarify the ambiguity surrounding controversial issues such as affirmative action and minority business contract set-asides. It can also help managers explain their policies to stockholders, employees, customers, suppliers, creditors, regulators, journalists, and others.

Many executives want to do something constructive about race, but in their natural desire to avoid controversy, their efforts are greatly hampered. They understandably seek to ward off attacks from their constituents who resent social initiatives that they see as somehow unfair to them. Executives therefore have to balance conflicting interests and find compromises, an effort that requires a discerning social sense and solid judgment. Most managers, however, cannot convincingly explain their corporate social- and race-related policies. They want to help solve education, health, housing, employment, and other problems, but they usually only come up with hackneyed rhetoric and corporate-speak clichés about being "good corporate citizens" and "good neighbors" in communities where they have plants and headquarters. Corporate community relations and philanthropy should be based on solid principles. Restitution theory can become the basis for effective social investment and human resources policy.

SOCIAL ACCOUNTING

Race and class issues have a powerful impact on the economy, but since they cause almost universal nervousness, they are inadequately discussed. We cannot solve the other issues that concern us until we are clear about race. Our social and national income accounts do not shed the necessary light on these matters. Millions of discriminatory and exploitative transactions occur each year, but they are either not recognized at all or are improperly accounted for. We have begun to recognize and highlight such problems in other policy matters. For example, economists account for externalities in pollution and environmental damage from industrial and agricultural carelessness. In addition, they are beginning to come to better understand wealth and income transfers between generations.[5] Something like that goes on in the social sector as well. It is a kind of social pollution. These transactions include exclusionary discrimination and exploitative employment decisions, and similar harmful practices in education and training, lending, housing, and elsewhere. We do not understand the full impact of these events on the economy. Nevertheless, they profoundly affect overall economic performance, and they should explicitly be recognized and measured. At first, the processes may be crude; later, they can be refined in order to improve understanding and management of the economy.

This kind of analysis raises questions most would prefer to avoid. But refusing to acknowledge what is intuitively obvious and self-evidently just increases the chances of running the economy even further into dangerous waters.

RESTITUTION AND COMPASSION

Since the 1970s compassion has become a favorite buzzword of politicians, especially in presidential primaries. It was frequently heard in the 1988 primaries. Even some conservatives like columnist Kevin Phillips, for example, claim that conservatives are increasingly recognizing that Social Darwinism is not a sound premise for managing a modern, socially diverse, successful industrial nation. Even for them chronic gross inequalities are becoming unacceptable.

Racial discrimination in economic decisions helps generate inequalities in income and wealth distributions, contributing to the disproportionate shares of earned income enjoyed by the haves. It also helps explain why the have nots are disproportionately African American. Few among us believe that people who feel abused and cheated will work hard, be diligent, obey the law, stay in school, delay having children and then raise them carefully and attentively, cooperate, and self-improve. As long as that remains true, these people will be a drag on the economy, hurting private savings and investment and adding to the public costs of running cities, states, and the national government. Those who impose unjust arrangements on others ultimately pay a price, although they don't fully realize it or discuss it honestly. Restitution theory helps organize thinking on a number of puzzling issues. We often hear, for example, that the major political parties are grasping for ideas, or are out of touch with the American people. This is code language for the politicians' fear to tackle redistributive issues, especially when they have a racial dimension.

Certainly, few politicians will immediately embrace restitution theory as a way to approach problems, but, in time, discussion of public policy will be incomplete and defective without it.

ECONOMIC PRINCIPLES

Economic policy should be based on solid, widely accepted principles. In the case of the United States, these principles are free markets, competition, and private property; these three principles serve as the bulwark for U.S. policy. To these we can now add one more: the prevention of discrimination, exclusion, and exploitation, and their remedy when they do occur.

For over seventy years, socialist regimes passed up the practical value of private enterprise, free markets, individual risk and reward, and the power of private capital to benefit an entire society. Under Mikhail Gorbachev, the former Soviet Union finally turned to a free market economy, and the Eastern Bloc, too, repudiated their previous thinking about how to organize society. It is a nearly universal hope that this whole region will successfully work out the political and economic reforms over the 1990s. As for our own reforms, let's be candid. Capitalist societies, like the former Communist world, have been obtuse and recalcitrant about facing unpleasant realities. Free capitalistic processes are effective in enhancing the material well-being of the masses by encouraging individual effort, imagination, and production, but these activities also include inherent injustices.

Multiracial capitalist societies especially tend toward maldistributed income and wealth.[6] Their cultural and racial hierarchy is based not on fair competitive outcomes, but on unjust misuse of coercive power by dominant groups against others—as members of groups, not simply as individuals.

Free markets tend to produce systematic wealth accumulation based on racial, religious, and other discrimination, but this injustice can be minimized and corrected. While injustice comes in many forms, we are concerned here with systematic injustice of the type often loosely called exploitation. The fact is that investors, owners, managers, employers, highly skilled operatives, financiers, and other decision makers often, knowingly or otherwise, injure other people. Discriminatory decisions are part of many economic processes, but when this is pointed out, defenses are raised and countercharges are often hurled. Restitution theory permits an orderly, constructive discussion of exploitation.

Other forms of discriminatory injustice also deserve attention. Religious, ethnic, age, and gender discrimination continue to be destructive generally while benefiting selected classes. By examining racial injustice in this way, we open the door to the use of similar analyses and information to remedy other forms of economic injustice. Shedding light on the consequences of discrimination in this way is therapeutic.

WHAT IS TO BE DONE?

The American economy is still strong enough to generate new businesses, technical innovations, and new products, services and jobs at an impressive rate. In many ways it remains a worthy model for the world. But it also has worrisome sectoral and structural weaknesses. These retard growth, innovation, international competitiveness, and job creation. One reason for these defects is chronic injustice, for it undermines growth, diversification, and renewal.

Through our computers and improved theory and quantitative technique, past economic relationships can be reconstructed and audited, and economic injustice can be measured in ways that will help us correct it. But, we do not seem to recognize that injustice produces moral debts that can be measured and paid off through income and wealth redistribution. The result of paying these debts will be enhanced general performance.

Widespread feelings of injustice foster resentment, destroying mutual respect between leaders and followers and corroding the economy. It destroys the bonds needed to build respect and mutual support. We cannot generate and sustain economic progress if too many people feel the system is unfair and they are victims of a massive historic injustice that could be corrected if the majority wanted honorable dealings.

Everyone must be drawn into the work force, and they must be helped to grow, produce, achieve, and feel satisfied, proud, and valued. We can help the have nots learn and accept mainstream values and standards of conduct—courtesy, order, civility, and responsibility. Church, family, and school used to do the job well, but they have greatly weakened in recent years. We can help these institutions by investing in education of all kinds, and doing that will help pay the debt. The legendary Charlie Brown put it this way. "There's no problem so complex and fundamental that we can't just walk away from." Perhaps that is the way to handle our economic distress and its causes. In effect, that is what we've been doing, but it is not working. Continuing deterioration is the price we pay. So it is better to face the issues and find remedies.

We are approaching consensus on technical solutions. Savings, investment, training, education, labor, trade, antitrust, tax and capital formation, banking, science, and technology—all are receiving significant attention. Before the 1990s end, we might agree on what to do about most of those concerns. Technological improvements will continue to offer great benefits in every sphere. Nuclear fusion, superconductivity, lasers, ceramic technology, bioengineering, and computer advances will create better life chances for billions of people all over the world. They may also help save us from our institutional and political mistakes. But economic advance requires that we attend to our many problems. The schools are turning out too many ill-prepared graduates. Factories are too often idle, under capacity, or obsolete. Our buses, subways, parks, freeways, and downtown streets are too dangerous. Taxes unavoidably support the wretched. While we will never have utopia, we can change this scenario and make our neighborhoods, cities, regions, and the nation generally more to our liking.

Unfortunately, many haves continue to favor exploitative arrangements. As a result, their wealth and income is in part illegitimate, unjust, and ill gotten. As the political majority and swing vote, the middle classes refuse to support reform. They oppose capital redistribution, and they decline to tax and spend adequately for housing, health, education, more humane prisons, and the kind of training that would improve the lot of the have nots. By taking this attitude, the middle classes unwittingly prolong and deepen the agony.

RESTORATION

Income and wealth is grossly maldistributed. The haves receive too much, and the haves nots, too little, a situation that can be traced in part to unjust, wrongful means of misappropriation. Its persistence demoralizes, angers, and corrupts, and it menaces our economic performance. We can first monitor and measure what is wrong; then we can use taxes and budgets to mend the damage.

The haves want a stable, creative, orderly, efficient, internationally competitive, and just society. Consensus has been reached on our broadly shared national objectives: control inflation; hold down and reduce deficits; create employment opportunities for everyone; provide good health care for all; provide peace of mind as well as a comfortable retirement and old age; ensure personal safety and public order everywhere without greatly sacrificing traditional liberties; become more competitive in global markets; hold our own against our main competitors; keep interest rates low; increase self-sufficiency in energy; improve productivity; strengthen agriculture; and preserve rural opportunities and values; preserve healthy, intact families; protect our natural environment and restore it where it has been damaged; explore and use outer space; enhance science and technology and maintain leadership in creativity; defend our country and our allies; protect the financial system; stimulate savings and investment to upgrade housing, modernize plant and equipment, and draw capital into innovative industries and small businesses; and broaden opportunities for everyone to participate, contribute and benefit from all those successes. We can achieve these goals only if we face our obligations to help all members of society to participate fully.

1

Measuring the Social Debt

Descended from the apes! My dear, let us hope that it is not true, but
if it is, let us pray that it will not become generally known.
—The wife of the Bishop of Worcester,
speaking of Darwinism

Fellow Citizens. We cannot escape history.
—Abraham Lincoln

When it becomes generally known that the haves owe the have nots
trillions of dollars, it will likely produce short-run grumbling, but the
information will have long-run beneficial value. In 1987 the American
Council on Education and the Education Commission of the States created
a Commission on Minority Participation in Education and American Life
to review educational progress over the previous twenty-five years. The
commission included Gerald Ford, James E. Carter, Cyrus Vance,
Edmund Muskie, William P. Rogers, Thornton Bradshaw, Henry
Cisneros, and Benjamin Hooks, among others. Its report, *One-Third of
a Nation* found uneven or no progress generally and warned that, in some
respects, the gaps were widening. The *New York Times* headlined the
report this way: "Study Calls U.S. a Country Deeper in Debt to
Minorities."[1] Unfortunately, that phrase, "Deeper in Debt," was not
understood or meant literally.

A ROUGH IDEA

Let's put the debt in perspective. The following facts illustrate the
relative standing of the haves and have nots and of blacks and whites.

During the 1970s, 1980s, and into the 1990s, these relationships shifted up or down slightly but generally held. According to economist Andrew Brimmer writing in *Black Enterprise* magazine, by 1992 there were 13.5 million African Americans in the labor force, but they held only 12 million jobs; the remaining 1.5 million were unemployed. They constituted 10.8 percent of the total labor force of 125 million and 10.1 percent of the 118 million employed persons. But they were 22 percent of all unemployed workers, a rate of 10.7 percent, about twice the rate for all workers.

Brimmer also found that in 1985 African-American income was $192.4 billion, with total U.S. income $2.6 trillion, for a share of 7.3 percent.[2] Had African Americans received income in proportion to their population share, it would have been $319 billion rather than $192.4 billion. Or, if we use labor force participation share, their income would have been $282 billion. Thus, the income shortfall for that one illustrative year ranged from $67 billion to $127 billion, depending on how it is estimated. By 1990 black aggregate income had risen to $267.4 billion. Had it reached either income or labor rate parity, in that year they would have received $123.6 billion more.[3] The primary consideration in all these statistics is that about half that gap is caused by discrimination,[4] and that gap represents a benefit to the haves. Haves benefit from discrimination not only passively and indirectly, but also tangibly and materially, even though in most cases they do not themselves discriminate.

The white to black median income relationships have held since World War II at about 60 percent. In 1992 white median was about $36,000 and black about $21,000.[5] By 1992 the top 1 percent of households, 2.5 million people, earned as much in one year as the bottom 100 million people. Earlier, in 1989, after taxes the top 20 percent earned 49.7 percent, the middle 60 percent, 46.9 percent, and the bottom 20 percent, 4.3 percent.[6] In a recent representative year, 1987, 23 percent of families earned over $50,000; 20 percent earned $35,000 to $50,000; 27 percent from $20,000 to $35,000; 19 percent from $10,000 to $20,000; and 12 percent under $10,000.[7]

And what about wealth? In 1984 black wealth, as net worth, was $208 billion. That is 3 percent of the total U.S. wealth of $6.9 trillion. African Americans had received 7.2 percent of total money income, so their wealth share was even more out of line with their proportion of the population or of the labor force. Black people make up 9.5 million households out of the total 86 million households in the United States. If they owned 11 percent of total wealth, their net worth would have been $760 billion. Instead, it was $208 billion—$552 billion less than they should have held under these assumptions.[8] According to Swinton, about 50 percent of this gap can be attributed to past discrimination. Swinton's work at the Urban Institute and at the Southern Public Policy Center in Atlanta is the basis for this estimate. He found that the other 50 percent of the gap is due to differences in educational quantity and quality, age, location, and "culture," and possibly, too, to certain inherited characteristics that influence ability to perform. Median black family wealth is only 9 percent of median white wealth. That gap, more dramatically than the income gap, reflects processes that produced the social debt. The reason for much of that discrepancy is historic injustice.[9]

Now, let's look at human capital. A quick estimate reveals $30 trillion to be the present discounted value of the stream of lifetime earnings of the labor force. The black share of that will also fall short of the share that would have been expected under fair circumstances—by several trillion dollars in fact. This gap is the result of past injustices in investment in education and training.

In 1991 the Supreme Court reviewed Mississippi's misallocation of funds between white and black universities for generations. Such differential investments in education, out of a common resource pot, forcibly and wrongfully produces an unjust enrichment for whites at the expense of blacks. All across the country, north and south, similar processes and similar exploitative funding formulas hold in education and in on-the-job training. They diverted to whites expenditures that should have gone to blacks. Thus, a portion of white human capital, expected earnings, represents an unjust enrichment. It is part of the social debt.

The Commerce Department estimates physical total wealth at about $13 trillion.[10] But this does not properly reflect human capital.

IN THE BALLPARK

The social debt ranges from $4 million to $10 trillion.[11] By comparison, in 1991 Americans owed $729 billion in consumer debt and $2.4 trillion in mortgage debt. The racial gap in income and wealth is not simply lost resources. It represents values diverted to others, who receive an unjust benefit. This benefit accumulated and compounded, and was then bequeathed to present recipients. We can choose any time period and apply any of several techniques. The point is that injustice—specifically, discrimination and exploitation—produces benefits that can be estimated.

THUROW'S TECHNIQUE

In 1969 Lester Thurow published *Poverty and Discrimination*,[12] a landmark study that has received too little attention. He estimated that annually whites gained $15 billion, plus or minus $5 billion from employment discrimination. Few people noticed his finding, however, and so it did not affect public opinion. Although it had little influence on corporate policy and practice, it is critical to any understanding of our racial quandary and our productivity and competitiveness problems.

In 1969, at the Schools of Business at the University of California at Berkeley, under a research program on community economic development, Gerald Udinsky and Bernadette Chachere expanded on Thurow's work. Using a conservative 3 percent interest rate and adjusting for price changes, they found that from 1930 through 1968 discrimination benefited whites by $350 billion. The present value of that benefit is now over $600 billion.[13] Let's look at this approach to estimating current benefits from past unjust exclusion. There are many other ways to estimate these benefits, but Thurow's model is a good illustration.

This exercise is not the last word on estimation, but it serves the important function of showing that discrimination yields benefits. To exactly whom, and how, needs to be examined more precisely. The illustration opens the issue, allowing us to consider race, poverty, and economic performance in more useful ways, and suggesting creative policy possibilities.

FORMS OF DISCRIMINATION

Economic discrimination can take many forms.[14] First, there's *wage discrimination*. Employers have often paid blacks and whites differently, even though they were in the same occupation and had received the same education and training. Where quality of education is demonstrably different, as reflected in work performance, differing pay can be defended, unless the pattern is systematically different by race. In that case questions may be raised about why investment in education was discriminatory in the first place.

Second, there's *occupational discrimination*. Historically, employers channeled blacks into lower paid occupations. Given blacks and whites with the same education, training, and experience, and exerting the same effort, blacks were relegated to lower paid occupations, which we call occupational discrimination.

Third, we have *educational discrimination* as evidenced by underinvestment in black education. It is difficult to estimate the differences in the quality of black and white education. As many point out, the quality of time spent in school is generally ignored when we merely measure quantity, years spent in school. But the decisions to offer lower quality education to African Americans, to hold down their expenditures per pupil, to skimp on budgets for their schools, and to do all that in order to put more resources into white schools were made by those who benefited or by their representatives on their behalf. The end result is a large diversion of income and wealth, an unjust enrichment. If we are to hold to our announced ideals and principles of fairness, it has generated a wrongful current benefit.

SUMMARIZING THE MODEL

We find part of the social debt by determining average white income and then subtracting what it would be if whites were distributed in jobs in the same proportion as the total population, white and nonwhite. This difference is then applied to the total white labor force. That gives the dollar benefit from disproportionate access to good jobs and education, denied to blacks. Then we compare average white income and total income. In that case, the difference is applied to the total number of white workers. That tells us what white total income would be if whites were distributed according to our expressed ideals of fairness and did not enjoy the advantages that discrimination offers. Occupational discrimination leads to reduced competition for higher paying jobs. That obviously increases the incomes of those who are given those jobs over what it would otherwise have been.

Fourth, *employment discrimination* results when blacks are underrepresented among the employed. During recessions in particular, blacks tend to be first fired and last hired. During upswings throughout most of our history, unemployed whites have tended to be the first rehired.

The total employment rate is the rate whites would experience if there were no employment discrimination in their favor. The difference between white employment rates and total employment rates gives us the resulting estimate of how much this kind of discrimination benefits the favored groups. Then we estimate the income that whites would have lost if they were unemployed at the same rate as the total population, as well as the income lost by whites who were actually unemployed.

The white loss would have been greater had they been unemployed at the general unemployment rate rather than the protected rate. Thus, the unfair benefit here is the difference between the large hypothetical loss (had whites been unemployed at the same rate as the total population) and the smaller actual loss experienced by unemployed whites.

Finally, the benefits have been capitalized to tell us the present value. Next, we express the results in terms of recent prices. The value of the benefits from wage, occupational, and employment discrimination, for the sample of years 1929 to 1968, was over $600 billion in 1992. If we then extended this analysis back to 1885, 1785, or 1685, the amounts would be in the trillions. Table 1.1 and Figures 1.1 and 1.2 are based on the research begun at the Office of Urban Programs at the Business School, University of California, Berkeley.[15]

SHEDDING LIGHT ON INJUSTICE

Until recently we couldn't get a handle on these issues; only rough estimations and simple back-of-the-envelop estimates were possible. Now,

Table 1.1
Estimated Benefits from Labor Market Discrimination, 1929–1984

	From Wage and Occupation Discrimination	Extrapolated	From Employment Discrimination	Cap Rates	Summed	Present Value
1929	2.508	.086	3.966	6.272	19.0	
1930	2.178	.332	3.135	6.227	18.8	
1931	1.725	.487	3.239	6.039	18.2	
1932	1.236	.519	3.673	6.936	20.9	
1933	1.164	.527	3.794	5.132	20.4	
1934	1.430	.562	2.843	5.776	23.2	
1935	1.653	.611	2.480	6.500	26.0	
1936	1.878	.597	2.339	7.089	28.4	
1937	2.126	.583	2.313	7.445	29.7	
1938	1.947	.708	2.166	7.396	29.6	
1939	2.097	.691	1.995	7.767	27.9	
1940	2.343	.696	1.870	8.466	29.3	
1941	2.991	.439	1.730	6.296	20.3	
1942	3.894	.288	1.881	9.650	28.5	
1943	4.802	.123	1.841	10.604	29.4	
1944	5.113	.065	1.800	10.881	29.5	
1945	5.028	.128	1.737	10.562	27.9	
1946	5.002	.273	1.611	9.672	22.0	
1947	5.433	.317	1.596	9.427	23.7	
1948	6.053	.268	1.619	9.712	23.5	
1949	5.829	.262	1.543	9.358	24.2	
1950	6.401	.397	1.511	10.366	23.0	
1951	7.395	.243	1.540	10.913	22.2	
1952	7.730	.386	1.527	11.344	22.2	
1953	8.044	.274	1.547	11.519	21.9	
1954	7.972	.827	1.403	12.010	23.1	
1955	8.705	.779	1.439	12.760	22.9	
1956	9.191	1.022	1.354	13.288	23.5	
1957	9.555	.826	1.440	13.021	22.5	
1958	9.600	1.276	1.401	13.301	23.1	
1959	10.400	1.381	1.431	14.181	23.3	
1960	10.786	1.453	1.360	14.490	23.3	
1961	11.08	1.516	1.307	14.727	22.2	
1962	11.84	1.626	1.262	15.566	23.1	
1963	12.49	1.742	1.217	16.234	23.0	
1964	13.41	1.633	1.177	17.313	23.4	
1965	14.60	1.208	1.129	17.433	22.1	
1966	16.10	1.351	1.081	18.753	22.5	
1967	16.92	1.457	1.049	19.160	22.5	
1968	18.50	1.620	1.00	20.12	22.4	
1969				20.00	18.4	
1970				19.75	18.7	
1971				19.50	18.5	
1972				19.25	19.3	
1973				19.00	20.1	
1974				18.75	19.7	
1975				18.50	19.2	
1976				18.25	19.9	
1977				18.00	20.1	
1978				17.75	21.5	
1979				17.50	21.9	
1980				17.25	21.4	
1981				17.00	21.7	
1982				16.75	20.8	
1983				16.50	21.4	
1984				16.25	22.5	
					1277.7	−$638.50

1969–1984, assumed annual incremental decline in discrimination for the purpose of these rough estimates.

Figure 1.1
Benefit from Employment Discrimination

U   total unemployment rate

U^w white unemployment rate

LF^w white labor force

I^n black average income

B^u benefit from employment discrimination

$$B^u = [(U \times LF^w)] - [(U^w \times LF^w)] \; I^n$$

Figure 1.2
Estimating Benefits from Race Discrimination
Benefits from wage and occupational discrimination

$$B = \sum_i \left[\sum_{jk} \frac{P^w_{ijk}}{P^w_i} I^w_{ijk} - \sum_{jk} \frac{P_{ijk}}{P_i} I_{ijk} \right] P^w_i$$

was used to determine the Benefit where:

P_{ijk} = total employed, sex i, occupation j, and education k

P^w_{ijk} = white employed, sex i, occupation j, and education k

$P^w_{i.}$ = white employed, sex i

P_i = total employed persons, sex i

I_{ijk} = average income, sex i, occupation j,
       and education k, and

I^w_{ijk} = white employed average income, sex i, occupation j, and
       education k

however, we can refine these measurements and generate better numbers. The reasons are that we have better economic theory to explain the workings of labor markets, better census and other data, better statistical technique, and, most important, computers. Without modern computers, the estimates would be impossible, even if we had decent data, theory, and technique. Today, we can do historical reconstructions and retroactive audits, so that we can at least discover the general magnitudes of the consequences of economic injustices. We could monitor it weekly or monthly and announce the findings regularly. With that kind of measurement, injustices would shrink dramatically because they thrive when they cannot be measured nor fully and widely understood.

As long as the victims of broad systemic injustices could only grouse about being treated unfairly, they could not consistently generate corrective political or other action. Now that we do have the ability to constantly measure injustice, what then? When victims discover not only that they are victims, but also who benefits and by how much, that knowledge will have extraordinary cleansing and corrective effects. Turning the spotlight on what happens to the fruits of injustice will help us correct it and minimize future injustice. The whole truth will gradually emerge.

In *Maximum Feasible Misunderstanding* (1970)[16] Daniel P. Moynihan reminds us of John Kenneth Galbraith's observation that statisticians are key in social policy and social change. That's because frequently only when we have learned to measure complex problems can we generate broad political interest and support for solutions. Of course, we still talk about discrimination and other deeply ingrained injustices as if they were simply not nice— "lamentable, but that's human nature." As for measuring them, well, it's like white-collar productivity: it can't be measured, or so we are told. But that just isn't true. The measures may be crude but they are useful and adequate for improving how we evaluate options for managing the problems.

THROUGH INJUSTICE, WE HAVE SHOT OURSELVES IN THE FOOT

In 1986, Japan's prime minister Nakasone, caused a flap when he ignorantly and chauvinistically stated that the United States' ethnic diversity, including many African and Hispanic Americans, was a competitive handicap and lowered overall productivity. After he was jumped on in the press, he felt compelled to clarify what he "really meant." Again, in 1991, other Japanese political and business leaders let the cat out of the bag and spoke of their private views on American weakness, lack of work ethic, and ethnic defects.

Were they entirely wrong? African Americans, on average, have been undereducated, but why? The reason was not simply that whites wanted to dominate blacks; rather the reason was more complex. Although there were scarce resources for human development, all the decision makers were white and they consistently decided to misallocate wrongfully and coercively, disproportionate shares of those resources that the labor of all the people had produced. As one result, many blacks cannot make a full contribution. That will be true until that current shortfall in human capital development and educational investment has been corrected and the debt paid.

INCOME AND WEALTH

In the 1980s, 90 percent of Americans enjoyed at least some increase in income.[17] This is a relative issue, however. From 1980 to 1988 the income of the top 10 percent grew 27.4 percent. The top 5 percent was up 37.3 percent to a median of $124,651, and the top 1 percent grew by 74.2 percent from $174,498 to $303,900. Some defended that disproportionate growth as being a due reflection of their disproportionate contribution of talent, risk taking, creativity, hard work, and leadership in the economy. But it also reflects some unjust enrichment. The top 1 percent of families control more wealth than the bottom 90 percent.[18] A portion of the $7.5 trillion net worth of the top 10 percent can be traced to exploitative past relationships. By 1986 median white household net worth was $39,135, and black was $3,397.[19] In addition, 30.5 percent of the 9.5 million black households had $0 or negative net worth. Only 8.4 percent of the 25.3 million white households were in that fix, however.

It is also worth noting that the top 30 percent did include African Americans. By 1970, 15.7 percent earned over $35,000. And by 1986, 21.2 percent were in that bracket in constant dollars.[20] And 8.8 percent earned over $50,000. Nonetheless, the top 30 percent, the haves, is overwhelmingly and disproportionately white. By 1986, 25 percent of all households earning over $48,000 had median net worth of $123,474, but they accounted for 38 percent of total family net worth.

All these numbers from the past ten years reflect centuries of distortions in market transactions and in education. They are evidence of a pattern of injustice resulting in lopsided and unstable prosperity.

2

Viewing Social Policy Through the Restitution Lens

All I want to say is, I don't think I owe blacks anything after what happened to my grandaddy during Reconstruction. And my daddy was a sawmill man. He took care of lots of black families during the Depression. Yes, he did.

> —A seventy-two-year-old volunteer in SAVE (Selma Area Voter Enlistment), a 1984 registration campaign

I'll never owe nothing to a black except a whippin'. And I always pay my debts!

> —Dialogue from *Roots*, January 1977

Now that we have outlined restitution theory, we have one way of measuring the social debt, and we can apply it to opinions in the press, to scholarship, and to management and practical affairs. In this chapter, we look at social policy through the restitution lens. Viewed from the perspective of the restitution theory, much opinion and comment on race and poverty are irrelevant, irrational, incomplete, or flawed in other ways, and even indefensible. Restitution theory also allows better officiating in the social ballgame. Many advocates of conflicting points of view will want to kill the umpire who calls balls and strikes conscientiously, but social income accounting will help public and corporate decision makers make sounder policy.

RUMORS OF INFERIORITY

Many people believe African Americans are disproportionately poor, not because of past discrimination and slavery, but because they are, on average, genetically deficient. The *New Republic*, the *Public Interest*, and *Commentary Magazine*, among others, have subtly tried to advance this idea. The apparent motive is to establish inferiority as the reason for income and wealth inequality. That would nullify claims for compensatory redistributive justice based on restitution. The fact is that scientists have no solid evidence for the belief, and its credibility diminishes as more African Americans who receive quality education compete effectively in the work world.

During most of America's history, discrimination against African Americans has been thorough and severe; only since about 1965 has it relaxed significantly. Our short memory, or, in some cases, our selective amnesia, renders us unable to face those facts and to allow the have nots to contribute and enjoy their earned rewards. In recent decades themes such as Crime in the Streets, No More Quotas, Preferences or Set-Asides, Welfare Queen and Willie Horton have swayed voter opinion in a major way, but restitution theory will make such tactics less effective.

COMMON FIRST REACTIONS TO RESTITUTION THEORY

In 1971 the Center for the Study of Democratic Institutions, in Santa Barbara, California, provided an early forum for discussing the concept of restitution. The fellows who attended the meeting were on average liberal in political orientation. The president of the Center, Robert Hutchins, had been dean of Yale Law School and then president of the University of Chicago. I was invited to attend on the basis of an article I had written on the restitution concept. Dr. Hutchins listened politely to the presentation and then responded: ''My great grandfather helped escaping slaves to freedom on the Underground Railroad. I don't see why I owe anyone anything.'' In my experience, this has been the nearly standard first response from liberals and conservatives alike: they feel they have done their part and nothing else is owed.

THROUGH THE RESTITUTION LENS

Viewing social commentary through the social debt lens clarifies social policy dilemmas. That normal first response to restitution theory is often exasperation—that they've had enough, are fed up with rehashing the past, and there should be a cut-off point, some kind of statute of limitations. People should stop dwelling on centuries-old grievances and the United States' success derives in part from the people's willingness to forget old grievances and their lack of obsession with the past which still hampers Europeans.

They often concede that white Americans treated the Indians badly, but need not pay reparations by giving back territory. They acknowledge that slavery remained a burden, but that while the United States should not deny its past and responsibilities, it should not argue them neurotically.

Many people express this same opinion when they first hear about restitution theory. Perhaps, they say, we should acknowledge a debt and offer some recompense as a goodwill gesture, but then it would be best to forget about it and move on. Fortunately, the choice does not have to come down to an irrational blood feud or quiet acquiescence. We have yet a third option: we can deal with the debt rationally and democratically.

Jean François Revel is concerned about the debilitating effects of guilt: "A civilization that feels guilty for everything it is and does and thinks will lack energy and conviction to defend itself when its existence is threatened."[1] Emotional guilt is not the point, however. The social debt is a practical issue. The American economy has been damaged by the burden of supporting the victims, for the contribution they could make has been lost. Moreover, their sullen resentment and sabotage have meant a great social cost.

Many Americans have come to internalize a bit of mistaken history about slavery without realizing the source. These erroneous opinions were first popularized by Ulrich Philips, a Yale historian of the 1920s. Although his ideas have long since been disproved, they are nevertheless still with us. For example, he stated that slavery was unprofitable and that it was untenable; in fact, he insisted, it would have been voluntarily phased out because it was not economically sound. He also believed that slavery contributed little to U.S. growth and prosperity.[2] Later researchers, including Alfred Conrad and John Meyer[3] and Roger Ransom and Richard Sutch,[4] have come to different conclusions. Robert W. Fogel and Stanley L. Engerman's famous work, *Time on the Cross* (1974), went to the heart of the matter. They found that in the late 1800s, "taxation and fiscal policies were used to transfer income from blacks to whites, perhaps more effectively, certainly more elegantly, than had been possible under slavery."[5] Fogel and Engerman also estimated the value of what they called "uncompensated pain and suffering" from bondage. But restitution theory does not address that notion, even though it is an element in other reparations theories.

"Okay," some might say, "I'm a second- (or third- or fourth-) generation American. I'm doing well. I'm a have. I see how maybe I'm part of a class that benefits collectively from twentieth-century discrimination, especially since my income is well in the top 30 percent, well over $40,000. But I can't understand how I benefit from slavery that occurred before my direct ancestors arrived here." Large quantities of free labor in the seventeenth, eighteenth, and nineteenth centuries were used to build infrastructure. Land was cleared, and roads, dams, levees, and ports were built. All that work, and more, was necessary to get the economy to the point that it needed and could absorb fresh immigration.

Slaves received food, clothing, shelter, and medical care, but they, in effect, paid high income taxes, all withheld. Although some of the "tax" went to the owner rather than to government, it was in a sense imposed on one race to benefit the working, middle, and upper classes in another race as well as their posterity.

Perhaps many Americans may conclude that, yes, this picture is accurate, and they may feel guilt about benefiting from such unfair economic arrangements. As observed earlier, however, arousing nonspecific emotional guilt is of little good and could even lead to a backlash. Obviously, Americans today are not guilty of slavery, and most do not consciously engage in direct economic racial discrimination. Still, they are caught up in the process as indirect and passive inheritors of the benefits of slavery and discrimination. The point here is that we cannot generate broad comprehensive prosperity until we see the connections between our affluence and others poverty, and between our problems and their plight.

Paul Weyrich, president of the Free Congress Research and Education Foundation, a New Right organization, has recognized a connection between the haves' well-being and the have nots' distress. In a 1987 report, "Cultural Conservatism: Toward a New National Agenda," he said, "Conservatives make a mistake in identifying with a politics that says it really doesn't matter what happens to the community as long as those who can survive get theirs."[6] He might resist the restitution idea, but he and other conservative elements might profit from looking at complex policy questions through the restitution lens.

A MORAL DEBT?

Is this a moral issues? Yes, of course it is. Most Americans consider slavery and discrimination both immoral and unjust, and agree that the practices have rightly been outlawed, even though subtle discrimination continues. The real question, however, is this: Is it moral to accept benefits from admittedly immoral practices of which we disapprove? This should be our concern, and not merely the immorality of historic practices themselves. We also should not dwell on the noneconomic psychic and cultural effects of past relations. Nor should we beat our breasts about the middle passage and about lives lost or damaged. Let us focus on what we can remedy as a practical matter and concentrate on current measurable benefits. That is where common sense suggests real policies can lead to real differences in peoples' lives.

Harvard's Robert Nozick has neatly rebuffed most objections to restitution theory.[7] He defines what he calls a distribution by legitimate means and claims that "justice in holdings" is historical. Not all current holdings, however, are produced in accordance with the two principles of justice in holdings: justice in acquisition and justice in transfer. In other words, some wealth was improperly acquired and bequeathed, that is, unjustly held.

What would be the current situation if something else had happened instead? We could speculate endlessly, for example, on what might have happened in North America, Europe, and Africa had there been no slavery, had it been different in character, had it ended earlier, or had restitution been made during Reconstruction. Engaging in such counter history only produces endless argument, however. What if Abraham Lincoln hadn't gone to the theater that night? That is interesting speculation, too, but to avoid unproductive directions, we focus on what *did* happen. What are the full consequences and how can we correct them to promote robust economic health in the 1990s?

WORK, FAMILY, AND FAITH

George Gilder says he believes that "the only dependable route from poverty is always work, family and faith. The first principle is that in order to move up, the poor must not only work, they must work harder than the classes above them. Every previous generation of the lower class has made such efforts. But the current poor, white even more than black, are refusing to work hard."[8] Hard work, family, and faith obviously have a lot to do with Americans' individual and collective progress. Indeed, the have nots certainly have to follow that prescription, but it's misleading to imply that African-American have nots have not already worked very hard. Most have, and so did their ancestors, even though it was on unfair, coerced, and illegitimate terms. Ironically, they thereby contributed to the advancement of many Americans into have status. The arguments of people like Gilder and Charles Murray[9] must especially be read through the restitution lens, for they would have us believe that the past is not prologue.

Stories about how nineteenth-century immigrants made it are often offered as a lesson to African Americans.[10] However, the analogy is bogus. Theodore Hershberg, a historian at the University of Pennsylvania, put it in perspective. Upward mobility, he said, was created by economic growth; that is how Irish, German, and other immigrants made it. This route has been more restricted for African Americans. In 1847, Hershberg points out, the average black worker in Philadelphia lived within a mile of 23,000 manufacturing jobs, "twice the number accessible to the typical Irish, German, or native white worker," but he was excluded. Blacks were *excluded* from new, well-paying jobs, *uprooted* from many traditional unskilled jobs, *denied* apprenticeships, and *prevented* from using the skills they had.

This same pattern, Hershberg noted, was repeated when "the next wave of immigrants—Italians, Poles, Slavs, and Russian Jews—arrived in

Philadelphia half a century later.'' The opportunities the Irish and Germans had in Philadelphia from 1885 to 1925 were boundless compared to those available to African Americans migrating from the South after 1945.[11]

RESTITUTION TO NATIVE AMERICANS

Many lawsuits have been filed for damages plus additional relief on behalf of many Indian tribes. When restitution to African Americans is discussed, a frequent response is, ''what about other people?'' Of course, restitution theory extends to other similar injustices. The real motive behind the question, however, is usually not how to address all injustices. Rather, it is to load on so many instances that it will be absurd and impractical to consider any claims. Then, none will be honored.

Restitution theory clearly fits Native American claims. Not only do formal legal bases exist for their lawsuits, but also Native Americans are entitled to a redistribution of capital. That redistribution would be based on injustices in the coerced and illegitimate expropriation of their territory and would extend beyond remedies available under specific treaties. In 1979, the U.S. Court of Claims ruled that the Sioux deserved $17 million for the land and 5 percent annual interest under the 1851 Fort Laramie Treaty. The court said there had been no good faith effort to award the Indians just compensation. Under Indian claims law, the $17 million can be awarded on the basis of the concept of the government's dishonorable dealing. Justice Blackmun, speaking for the Supreme Court majority, said that the lower court was correct in finding the subsistence rations given the Sioux paid only for depriving them of their chosen way of life, and were not intended to compensate them for the land taking.

Thus, Native Americans can obviously make a strong case for general restitution, as can many quasi-indigenous, that is, third-generation, Native Hispanics. These three groups have been here so long that they are all essentially indigenous relative to most other Americans.

HOW CAN WE AFFORD THAT?

Voters are frequently asked to state their preferences on policies that amount to restitution, but the issue is never put to them so directly. It is murky and is subject to political distortion. Policy choices often propose implicit or explicit redistribution from one class to another. Restitution theory can clarify these choices. Then the practical question becomes, What is the best way to pay the debt in these specific circumstances, given real-world constraints and risks?

RIGHT AND LEFT AGREE?

Charles Krauthammer is a columnist who is usually considered to be conservative, but in 1990 he explicitly called for reparations to African Americans. His figure was $100,000 for each family of four, as a one-shot deal; after that, there would be no more affirmative action or other "preferences."[12] His $100,000 figure is too low. Based on the estimates we've seen, it should instead work out to $300,000 to $400,000 per household. Although his method of payment is not sound, the spirit is. He clearly grasps the central element in restitution theory, but he might reject restitution explicitly proposed. Krauthammer says:

My American identity entitles me to . . . benefits. . . . (and obligations). I cannot claim one and disdain the other.

During . . . slavery in America, my ancestors were being chased . . . across Eastern Europe. . . . But . . . (to) be American today is to share in those obligations. . . . Collective responsibility is an elementary principle of national life.

THE UNDESERVING POOR

We frequently read a variant of the following news story. Irate neighbors are resisting a proposed public housing project, school program, or other government action. They insist that "It's not race. We just don't want our tax money going to folks who don't deserve or appreciate what they already get. And we don't want to support lazy good-for-nothings. Nobody gave us anything. We worked hard for what we have. Let them do the same." Or this: A panel of distinguished sociologists, economists, politicians, or business leaders discusses another public proposal: "The policies of the sixties failed. We learned you can't throw money at problems. You also can't ask government to do everything for everybody. You've got to curb expectations. The deficit, inflation, military preparedness, taking care of the middle class, and our trade balance are top priorities. We've got to balance the budget, cut taxes, cut government spending, reduce regulation, and increase productivity. Then everyone will benefit from growth. A rising tide lifts all boats." Each group and each point of view represents strong social longings and resentments. They also express a persistent impulse to maintain the existing distributions of income and wealth and to help only the "truly disadvantaged." When we view them through the restitution lens, however, these common attitudes are inadequate and flawed.

UNPRODUCTIVE RACIAL DIALOGUE

When we think and talk about race, poverty, injustice, and social problems, we talk past each other, and we base our views on assumptions that are poorly explained. The discussion leaves a deficient understanding of other points of view. Restitution theory clarifies grievances and optimal remedies by quantifying them.

Harvard's Nathan Glazer disagrees: "The fact is that we cannot separate ethnic and racial groups into two classes: those who have suffered, economically and culturally in America, and therefore deserve redress, and those who have not."[13] Donald L. Horowitz concurs. He says Glazer sees affirmative action as a threat to ethnic diversity and to the consensus that government would not act based on group characteristics. And "proponents of measures stronger than those fostering open opportunity should be put to a greater burden of justification than they have so far shouldered."[14]

In contrast, Robert Nozick says a debt may exist and should be paid. "People are entitled to what they have if they got it in a legitimate way. . . . The most serious intervention in the free labor market . . . was slavery. We're still bearing the consequences. . . . I think reparations may be in order. And Indians are another problem."[15]

RESTITUTION THEORY IS ULTIMATELY A MORAL ISSUE

In our legal tradition we have "inherited" liabilities along with our assets. Assets are bequeathed, but most liabilities must be honored and creditors satisfied before assets can be distributed to heirs. Slavery was legal for a long time; and economic discrimination, though largely illegal, has been widespread. Thus, we might object that, even if we do benefit from past economic injustices, those practices were accepted at the time. Making restitution so late is ex post facto and violates legal and constitutional principles.

Depending on its ideological composition, an appeals court might find that perspective technically correct. Thus, the concept might not prevail in such a court in a formal adversarial proceeding. As a practical and moral matter, however, we cannot have it both ways. If past practices are now seen as unacceptable and offensive, the benefits are illegitimate. Boris Bittker countered that objection by saying that "there is nothing remarkable in . . . redressing injuries attributable to acts thought to be legal when committed, if they are condemned by a later change in legal or constitutional doctrine."[16]

CAN'T WE LET BYGONES BE BYGONES?

Some time ago, the United States and India agreed to wipe out India's $3.2 billion debt from economic assistance contracts. It amounted to 20 percent of India's currency. Of the rupees granted outright to India, $1.3 billion were to go to agriculture; the rest was targeted for family planning, housing, education, health, electric power, and rural electrification. It made sense to set aside the Indian debt. Other international debts—to Israel, Egypt, Poland, and the like—have similarly been written off. With regard to our domestic social debts, however, we're better off recognizing, not forgetting, our obligations. We cannot let bygones be bygones.

WHAT ABOUT EVERYBODY ELSE?

Racial discrimination is one obvious example of economic injustice, but many Americans are descended from the victims of other kinds of discrimination. Many European Americans, as Glazer, Krauthammer, and Horowitz note, were also discriminated against. Their direct, actual ancestors were victims of the same or similar processes in Europe or here. Almost every ethnic group, tribe, or nation has at some time exploited another group or been exploited. Hence, in theory, there are debts all around. What about the descendants of the biblical Hebrews, for example? Shouldn't they make a claim against Egypt? And should the descendants of Roman slaves present a bill to modern Italy? It's hard to imagine a practical favorable result from any of those claims. In part, that's because those are ancient and international, not domestic, claims.

In the United States, restitution is feasible because, as a practical matter, we can respond democratically and put the issue before Congress, hold hearings, research it, debate it widely, and decide what to do. In contrast to the European immigrants and their descendants, Hispanic, Native, and African Americans, from the seventeenth through mid-twentieth centuries, encountered economic discrimination because of both class and race. As a result, their numbers among the have nots are disproportionally large. Hence, they are restricted in their ability to compete and produce, and thus it is that injustice that undermines the nation's total performance.

We need to help all the have nots so that they can contribute to society. This effort is hampered by a bad habit shared by many politicians, journalists, and social scientists. They tend to lump all the poor, or all the working class, or all the middle class together. This fudging of historic distinctions is misleading, inasmuch as each major class that has been victimized by dicriminatory injustice has had a different experience. These differences are worth noting. Social debts are obviously owed to Native Americans, as well as indigenous Hispanic Americans whose ancestors' and or labor, or both, were appropriated. Well, we might say, with Glazer, what about Appalachia? And what about other depressed agricultural, industrial, and mining regions? Those peoples' ancestors also lost income and wealth through industrialization and tax, tariff, and agricultural policies.

The answer is, let us invest in them and help them to live rich rewarding lives, but let us understand that there are different reasons for targeting programs to them. The scale and duration of the remedial programs should also be different because of the differences in historical background. Regional disparities existed, with many Scotch Irish, English, and other early immigrants finding themselves isolated or disadvantaged in rural and urban areas. Hershberg's findings are telling, however. They did suffer injustices as members of a class, but as white have nots. They were exploited because they were vulnerable and relatively immobile. Those who left depressed areas could prosper; those who remained poor were simply unable to fully capitalize on their relative racial advantage. Historically, most European immigrants of the nineteenth and early twentieth centuries faced comparatively brief institutionalized restrictions on their collective or individual progress. Their race was often an asset to them when they competed with African Americans. At worst, as Hershberg reminds us, it was never a liability.[17]

For Native, Hispanic, and African Americans, the situation was different, and it continued over very long periods. For these people race was an inherited bar to training, investment, participation, competition, accumulation, and upward mobility in general. It created legal arrangements that were specifically designed to increase their economic burdens. The African Americans' nationality, that is, the fact that they were Americans, had marginal value: it offered limited physical and economic protection, and in certain regions only. Their citizenship provided no material advantages, such as were enjoyed by most other citizens who were competing with noncitizen recent arrivals for jobs, education, housing, and training opportunities, or commercial credit. African Americans were readily displaced from both skilled and unskilled occupations, as well as from established business ownership, by newly arriving noncitizens. That unjust displacement, which took place during a period of rapid general growth and widening opportunity (1870–1940), diverted income and wealth from them to others. That process helped produce today's debt.

It is still true that nearly everyone has known injustice at some time. There are distinctions, however, and certain injustices can be assigned priority for correction. Therefore, we do not need to conclude that, since everyone has been harmed at some time, no one is entitled to a remedy unless everyone is simultaneously recompensed. That is the posture assumed by those who oppose government intervention in redressing any class injustices.

3

How to Pay the Debt

Getting into debt is a tanglesome net.
—Ben Franklin

. . . we shall all consider ourselves unauthorized to saddle posterity with our debts, and morally bound to pay them ourselves. . . .
—Thomas Jefferson

I've been poor and I've been rich. And, Honey, rich is better.
—Pearl Bailey

If we accept the proposition that the history of economic race relations produces a current measurable obligation, what should we do? If the debt is $4 to $10 trillion, how can it be paid? Here is one way to pay much of it over the next forty years through targeted programs that will benefit all Americans. These investments would be over and above current levels (all figures are in billions of dollars):

	Total	Annual
Quality housing	$1,000	$25
Quality education	1,000	25
Quality health	200	5
Quality training and employment	200	5
Quality corrections, rehabilitation, law enforcement, and behavior	200	5
Business capital	1,600	40
	$4,200	$105

To upgrade the have nots so that they can become full contributors, this tabulation gives us a rough idea of additional expenditures needed. Restitution theory states that African Americans would themselves have made these investments over the centuries in themselves out of normal earnings and savings. Instead, this money was coercively diverted to others. Obviously, they did survive slavery and discrimination and with income available to them they somehow acquired the basic necessities. Lost were the extra incremental earnings that they would have realized had they had full opportunity and access. This money would have flowed into quality education, housing, health, savings, and investment and would have resulted in quality assets and a quality way of life. That is precisely what paying the debt will accomplish. We should, therefore, pay these debts with careful investments in people and businesses.

But many object that "You can't just throw money at problems." We often hear that admonition during political campaigns. But what does it mean? Sometimes it means, "Be prudent and budget conscious. Don't burden taxpayers with wasteful programs." Or it means, "Don't fund new programs, wasteful or otherwise. No more social engineering. Don't change existing racial status relationships." Or it means, "Manage existing programs professionally. We've made mistakes. And taxpayers have a right to be concerned about how government approaches complex problems. We've produced too many unanticipated consequences." But often it means: "Let's keep the distributions of income and wealth as they are. Don't use public policy to close the racial gap."

Jack Kemp opposes redistributive proposals. He quotes William Bennett's claim that $2.6 trillion was spent to try to solve problems during the twenty years of the Great Society and the War on Poverty.[1] But that didn't work. What if that figure is correct? Suppose $100 billion a year was spent for twenty-six years? What was it spent on? Most of the programs which we think of as part of the War on Poverty, as well as related entitlements, were maintenance programs, not investments. They did not equip people to compete; rather they simply allowed them to survive. Moreover, much of the money went for administrative overhead. Therefore, assertions that massive spending did little good, that "The Great Society didn't work," are false. It was never seriously funded because the rationale was never solid.

HOW TO THROW MONEY AT PROBLEMS

While we need to throw money at some problems, we should pitch with pinpoint control. Let Tom Seaver rather than Don Larsen or Nolan Ryan pitch. They all pitched well, but Larsen holds the records for hit batsmen and wild pitches and Ryan walked a lot of batters. Seaver, or, earlier, Philadelphia's Robin Roberts, were models of control and accuracy. We need control and accuracy to design, fund, and manage social and developmental programs when we throw money at problems. To pay this social debt, we need to throw capital transfers, not subsistence income transfers. Quality training, education, business capital, crime prevention, housing equity, and wage subsidies are good ways to make restitution. Human capital as well as financial and physical capital transfers that build competitiveness and productivity are effective ways to repay. That will correct inequities in ways that contribute to overall economic performance. Thus, we also need to stimulate business development, along with investment in employment, training, education, behavior modification, housing, and health.

A RISING TIDE?

Many political leaders and economists believe that the poor can be helped simply by using a portion of income growth rather than through income redistribution. However, unless we create a more dynamic economy through creative public-private partnerships, we will have only limited growth. Part of the reason is that we waste the potential contributions of millions of have nots by depriving them of income they would recycle back into human capital and other general investments. Therefore, lagging growth and concerns about the rise of strong international competitors are partly a matter of the chickens coming home to roost. Faced with the reality of slower growth than in the period after World War II, what should the United States do? Simply put, a political consensus is needed to redistribute the pie. That will help accelerate growth by upgrading the have nots to full contributors. It is a practical matter, but the bottom line is moral. *It's the have nots' money.*

Redistribution is the way to pay what is owed, but critics will argue that redividing the pie damages rather than enhances overall incentives to participate and invest, and, therefore, will retard growth. That is how the debate shapes up.

INVEST IN HUMAN CAPITAL

High-quality preschool education works. This kind of investment is the best way to pay the social debt. Basic skills improvement, linking schools and local employers, and improving programs like the Job Corps will help solve unemployment problems for young people.

"BUT HAVEN'T WE PAID THIS DEBT ALREADY?"

The typical reaction, much like Jack Kemp's, is, "OK. The concept seems logical. And the accounting may be sound, although I want to see what others come up with. But here's what bothers me. Haven't we already more than paid that off? If there's a debt, the Great Society, the New Frontier, urban renewal, school lunches, welfare, have paid it.'' If this is an honest question, and not just a debating point, it deserves a real response. This debt results from income flows from accepted or officially sanctioned discrimination for 350 years. There have been flows the other way. We have government housing, health, welfare, education, employment, and business development programs. Don't the two flows more or less cancel one another?

Part of this debt has been repaid by government programs, but the haves tolerate most such programs as a price to be paid to sustain the have nots— but in their place. These programs are not designed or funded to produce real development. The haves don't want the have nots to slip too far. That could cause even worse social dislocation, and it would be too dramatically unfair and inhumane. They would live submarginal lives, which would be an unacceptable scenario. The haves tolerate these payments to help the unfortunate have nots maintain a bearable standard of living, but those payments should not be credited against the debt. Instead, we should count against the debt only programs that are constructive, rather than subsistence, that help strengthen the economy by strengthening the have nots. Only programs that upgrade earning power or provide a basis for personal or community growth and self-sufficiency count against the debt.

For example, we could guarantee a job to people if they promised to finish school and keep up attendance and grades. We could also guarantee a private or public job for people who have finished high school or equivalent training but can't find a job. The idea is to invest in quality education, training, health, home ownership, and business and economic development. But for the past thirty years, well-designed, sustained, well-managed programs at the right scale have been less common than poorly designed, poorly managed, underfunded, misdirected programs.

So, restitution theory has to overcome honest skepticism as well as ideological opposition. The debt can also be reduced with income maintenance or family assistance. Such investment would end at some point, say, in forty years, and if delivered in a disciplined way, combined with requirements to work and study, would make most have nots self-sufficient. High-quality law enforcement, crime prevention, rehabilitation, and corrections would also serve as remedial investment. It would strengthen communities and help individuals lead disciplined lives.

CUT WELFARE ABUSE AND DEPENDENCY

Paying the debt by helping the have nots in this way would improve their discipline, which is needed throughout society to have a smooth-working, competitive economy. But some social policies that have been in place for decades are counterproductive; some actually undermine discipline. Paying the debt in the right way—with developmental investments—will eliminate programs that destroy incentives, undermine families, and promote dependency.

Restitution theory poses an obvious danger: it might encourage some to believe the world owes them a living. Restitution is not an idea to be used cynically. Rather than justify parasitic predilections, it is designed to strengthen people willing to study, work hard, and lead disciplined, responsible lives. As a public policy concept, it can help decide how to stimulate the economy. Moreover, it points to policies that will strengthen poor and marginal people who cost taxpayers billions in wasted maintenance expenses but don't contribute.

Restitution does not justify malingering, trifling, idling, low productivity or "ripping off" employers or anyone. It is not an excuse for stealing, extortion, fraud, or rackets, and it cannot be used as a guilt trip.

Explicit debate on restitution and remedial income redistribution may exacerbate short-run hostilities. We can properly pay the debt not through welfare but through developmental investments. Those programs will strengthen the have nots and the economy generally.

Lester Thurow agrees that we should restructure income maintenance and welfare to stress employment, rather than subsistence transfer payments. In the early 1980s, for example, we spent only $10 billion to create jobs, but we spent $200 billion in transfer payments annually.[2] Jack Kemp would count those costs as developmental; they are not. In any event, that is not the right proportion. Restitution theory helps us target investment in employment and training to generate economic revitalization. That will have much greater payoffs.

PAY SOME OF THE DEBT BY INVESTING IN BUSINESS DEVELOPMENT

As a result of 370 years of exclusion from access to capital, technical and management training, and employment, a big wealth gap has been created in the United States between blacks and whites. Had that not happened, today there would be many more strong large, medium, and small businesses owned by African Americans. So one way to pay the debt is through capital subsidies and transfers.

All other restitution programs target the have nots, but this clearly has to benefit African Americans who are themselves haves, upper income, and highly educated. The rationale is that the businesses will strengthen the community and provide jobs; at any rate, they would have existed all along but for injustice. Such a serious, large-scale, sustained business development program will increase competition and will sharply enhance performance levels in industries where fresh ideas are needed. This is not largess; it is investment, and its justification is practical as well as moral.

Many special economic interests receive public support when they are considered to have a broad justification. Social groups have always been a focus for government economic policy. Paying the debt by subsidizing equity in companies owned by African Americans has sufficient precedent.

SUBSIDIZE ACQUISITIONS OF SMALL, MEDIUM, AND LARGE BUSINESSES

We can pay this debt, in part, by helping to create strong businesses. They would be bought, owned, and managed by people who had been unjustly excluded from business for many generations. Economic justice and a healthier economy will result if we provide capital subsidies to help African Americans acquire and develop businesses. Some will say that is not politically feasible, and some will not want government to subsidize such acquisitions no matter what the rationale. Obviously, given an easy choice, no one in a propertied position wants to give it up, but such transfers should be an element in a comprehensive economic revitalization program.

We can use a variation on the approach in federal urban renewal to help the social acquisition of businesses, or plants, or divisions of large companies. In urban renewal, the cost to acquire and prepare real estate usually exceeds the final sale price to developers. It is not uncommon for property to be disposed of for 50 percent of that total cost. The difference between total cost and disposition price is absorbed by the government. This subsidy to a private party is justified by the ultimate public purposes served by the development.

The same logic can apply to subsidizing purchases of going concerns as real property. Acquisitions occur everyday in the normal course of business, but a federal subsidy can help some of this steady turnover to flow to indigenous and quasi-indigenous minorities. For centuries, Native, African, and some Hispanic Americans were actively prevented from going into business, or witnessed the destruction of businesses they had started. This approach will help right that wrong. To do so, we can modify existing programs. It is simply a social variation on business assistance already offered. After, say, forty years, the procedure would be discontinued. By then, African, Native, and Hispanic Americans would be significant participants in enough industries.

Restitution is conceptually an excellent guide to social investment policy in business development of this kind. Paying most of the social debt through capital subsidies is crucial, and human capital programs—education and training—would be foremost. Other kinds of capital development should also be included. Manufacturing, transportation, merchandising firms, banks, and insurance companies can be acquired. In this way, fuller economic participation at a significant scale becomes possible.

This level of participation would have occurred naturally long ago had there been no economic injustice—no coerced income diversion, no discriminatory distortions in employment, savings, borrowing, and investment.

4

Creative Antitrust: Subsidized Social Divestiture

... the proper Constitutional objective of government is not to promote efficiency but to prevent the concentration of power.
— Louis Brandeis

Use of antitrust philosophy can help change the social-economic overconcentrations that have reduced the economy's efficiency and created an imbalance in social power. Although the United States is a racially diverse country, only one race controls every major industry and every major company. This situation originally arose in part because of distortions and social restrictions in commercial competition. Because many talented African Americans were wrongfully excluded from business, today the United States is a kind of social monopoly. This factor is in part responsible for our present economic weakness and the decline of whole economic sectors.

SUBSIDIZE THE ACQUISITION OF FIRMS THAT ARE DIVESTED THROUGH ANTITRUST ACTION

One way to pay some of the social debt owed is to modify antitrust policy so that social overconcentration can be remedied. Accordingly, African Americans and the other indigenous minorities would be able to bid for certain businesses. "Breaking up" some overconcentrated industries for social reasons would simply stretch a well-established antitrust precedent, and it would contribute to improved economic vigor and competition.

The U.S. economy is undermined by monopoly in the conventional sense, and it is damaged by social monopoly as well. Amending the

Sherman Antitrust Act would help preserve competition, protect small business, and accelerate participation by African-American businesses in sectors they have been excluded from. Social monopoly has the same anticompetitive and socially dangerous consequences as classical monopoly. It reduces overall efficiency by excluding people who would compete, and it concentrates too much power in one social group. Antitrust philosophy can embrace minority business development. For example, voluntary divestiture to minorities could be used as a legal defense. Firms such as Bank of America and Security Pacific, Chemical Bank and Manufacturers Hanover, Kraft and General Foods, R.J. Reynolds and Nabisco, Gulf + Western, Bendix, United Technologies, Textron, U.S. Steel and Marathon Oil could be required to spin off units when they seek court or regulatory approval for an acquisition or merger. This would be a reasonable way to get more competition.

THE FTC, THE DEPARTMENT OF JUSTICE AND PRIVATE SUITS

Antitrust legislation could help minority business development by leading to a gradual structural realignment whereby the present grossly disproportionate dominance by one racial group would end. Here, divesture means that in order to get permission to buy another company, a big company or a big bank, would have to sell off a small division, or subsidiary, or a number of branches. There is precedent for putting this widely understood concept into action. By using it in this new way, the structural problem of social monopoly could be remedied.

The extraordinary degree to which racial minority groups are excluded from production and investment is contrary to the public interest in our heterogeneous society. Indeed, market power is overly concentrated. Redistributing going concerns would help pay the social debt. Antitrust policy could reflect the broad policy objective of restitution through capital redistribution.

RACE AND COMPETITION

The gross underrepresentation of racial minority groups, industry by industry, suggests that the major industries are inherently racially exclusionary. Although antitrust is intended to promote competition, "normal fair" competition is itself restrictive because of pervasive bias. We therefore need to address this structural impediment so that all persons can fairly enter and compete. Monopoly presents barriers to entry, impedes innovation, distorts prices and restricts production. Racial monopoly clearly does, too.

DIFFICULTIES IN APPLYING EXISTING ANTITRUST LAW

Applying existing antitrust law to racial exclusion is not easily accomplished, for we should be careful in stretching statutes or principles designed for one purpose to cover different purposes. Our existing laws were not intended to apply to social monopoly or racial exclusion. Even applying antitrust principles to social exclusion, not to mention applying the actual law, presents a problem. The problem is, what was the intent or motive?

We might ask whether the actions leading to social monopoly were motivated by some kind of collective anticompetitive intent. In its defense, a hypothetical firm could simply ask "What racial discrimination? That was not a factor in our decisions." Thus, a formal antitrust approach requires proving culpable conduct and intent, an effort that prevents the use of traditional tools. Suppose we required government or civil rights groups or minority business plaintiffs to prove intent. That would prevent any intervention against institutionalized racial exclusion in normal business practice. Normal business tends to be racially exclusionary, as a result of which it is anticompetitive. However, it is difficult to use existing law to remedy it inasmuch as the law at present requires that culpable conduct be proved. How, then, could these minority groups use antitrust concepts to produce equal opportunities to compete in business? To do that, another approach is required.

THE STRUCTURAL APPROACH

We should look at the structure rather than the conduct of business so that we can incorporate social sensitivity into antitrust. Some industry structures in and of themselves—apart from how firms conduct themselves or their executives' intent—result in unacceptable concentration of power and opportunity for abuse. This undue market power can be curbed. In all major U.S. industries, the large corporations are owned by one majority racial group and minorities are grossly underrepresented. This kind of monopoly excludes fresh ideas and new approaches, and is a subtle but powerful cause of part of our inefficiency and lagging economic performance. We can require some divestiture, which would encourage breakthroughs to more competition and participation. The large enterprise is the sole domain of one race in the United States, a multiracial country. This structural fact makes normal business relations exclusionary in a broad sense in every industry and tends to hurt the economy. This excessive dominance presents an exclusionary high barrier to entry.

Even if this antitrust logic is accepted, caution is required. Government should not ask any company in any industry to voluntarily divest itself of divisions or product lines to minorities if the resulting new, free-standing, independent businesses will probably be weak. A program that creates weak competitors is hardly needed. With minority capital and experienced senior managers/operators in such short supply, divestiture should take place only if the results would make sense, and if minority owner/managers/investors are ready to meet the opportunity.

We might ask why there are so few minority-owned major corporations? Does overt discrimination explain it? But most overt actions that are economically exclusionary are covered by existing law. So what is the problem? The most persuasive explanation lies simply in the prevailing social patterns of ownership, which in and of themselves present exclusionary high barriers. It is for this reason that we have a social monopoly. The remedy can be found in establishing a program with two features: (1) major corporations in a socially overconcentrated industry would have to sell off units to minorities; and (2) major corporations that wanted to complete a merger would first have to sell off units to minorities.

AMENDING THE SHERMAN ACT

The Sherman Antitrust Act should be changed to help solve the problem of racial exclusion and monopoly and to encourage social divestiture. Following is a proposed revision of this law.

A BILL

To amend the Sherman Antitrust Act to include the treatment of social monopoly and to encourage the participation of indigenous and quasi-indigenous minorities—Pacific Islanders, Hispanic, Chinese, African, and Native Americans in business throughout American industry.

1. Be it enacted by the Senate and House of Representatives of the United States of America in Congress assembled that this Act may be cited as the Social Monopoly Act.

Title I. Findings and Purposes

Section 101. Findings
The Congress of the United States finds that
(1) American business is broadly characterized by exclusion of indigenous racial minorities from significant participation in most industrial sectors.
(2) There are, therefore, socially overconcentrated industries in which one racial group controls vastly disproportionate market and asset shares.
(3) There is a kind of persistent monopoly power by race. The "monopolists," in this case all major business decision makers as a class,

can be presumed to engage in deliberate conduct to maintain their advantage.

(4) The largest 2,000 corporations are owned and controlled entirely by one racial group, with gross underrepresentation of African-American and other minority racial groups. This is a market situation in which a racial group "jointly possesses undue market power."

(5) This situation presents an exclusionary high barrier to entry to indigenous Pacific Islanders, Chinese, Hispanic, African, and Native American firms.

(6) The prior absence of any larger minority firms tends to discourage subsequent entry and development of any other such firms at significant scale.

(7) The extraordinary degree to which these long-time resident racial minority groups are excluded from economic activity is contrary to the public interest in a heterogeneous society like the United States.

(8) The majority racial group holds an overwhelming degree of market power relative to these minority racial groups. Enhanced competition and participation are desirable. And racial factors in market composition can be taken into account.

(9) Antitrust policy can work to create and maintain equal opportunity in economic activity in these developing racial groups, and inhibit exaggerated levels of economic power in the majority racial group.

(10) The lack of ownership of larger corporations by African Americans and other minority racial groups suggests inherent racial exclusion in the structure of major markets.

(11) This apparently inherent bias in market structure restricts the participation of the indigenous minority racial groups.

(12) It is important to change the racial dominance of markets where feasible, so that all persons have an equal opportunity to compete.

(13) The concept of monopoly can be modified beyond its usual meanings. Monopoly impedes innovation, presents barriers to entry, distorts prices, and restricts production. It seems that social monopoly has the same consequences.

(14) Government can regulate monopolies, nationalize them, seek voluntary compliance with law, or use structural remedies.

(15) But it is difficult to apply existing law to racial exclusion in business of larger scale, and in most manufacturing, because it is difficult to show intent and culpable conduct. Therefore, if encouraging entry, sector by sector, is desirable public policy, there is a need for a new antitrust tool.

(16) Market structure rather than conduct is the proper focus in dealing with social overconcentration.

(17) The existing social overconcentration, in and of itself, and apart from the conduct of firms and business decision makers, results in unacceptable concentrations of social power and unacceptable opportunities for abuse

of majority racial and social status. The government can properly seek to curb such undue market power whether individually or jointly possessed.

(18) Persistent social monopoly power, as with traditional monopoly, in all but the most exceptional instances, can only be presumed to result from culpable conduct. In the case of social monopoly, however, the conduct has been almost universally perceived as normal.

(19) This social monopoly can be dissipated by requiring divestiture to indigenous minorities where such divestiture is practicable.

(20) In order for indigenous minority business to develop, there needs to be a structural realignment in markets characterized by this gross dominance by one racial group. This realignment should increase competition and efficiency.

(21) The total absence of indigenous minorities from any industry should be considered, on its face, as proof of unfair exclusion. If intentional efforts to exclude cannot be found to have caused the absence, then it can be concluded that market structure, per se, is the problem.

(22) It is possible through stimulation of divestiture and acquisitions to move toward a level of participation that would reduce to insignificance exclusionary barriers to entry.

Section 102. Purpose
Congress, therefore, declares that the purpose of this Act is to:

(1) Promote indigenous minority participation throughout the economy at every scale,

(2) Reduce barriers to entry to industry participation produced by social overconcentration of ownership and control of business concerns.

(3) Conduct systematic analyses of every major industry and pursue divestiture in those that are socially overconcentrated.

(4) In general, use structural remedies such as divestiture to promote socially open and free competition.

Title II. Amending Section 2 of the Sherman Antitrust Act

Section 201; Policy Objective of Title
The policy objective of this Act is the removal of barriers to entry to economic competition caused by social monopoly and social overconcentration of ownership and control of business assets.

Section 202. Amendment
1992—Every industry which shall be found to be monopolized by race, such that indigenous Pacific Islanders, Chinese, Hispanic, African, and Native American firms account for less than 5 percent of aggregate annual

sales, or less than 5 percent of assets, whichever is smaller, shall be deemed socially overconcentrated.

This condition shall be remedied,

(1) at the discretion of the Courts by means of negotiated divestiture to indigenous, that is, long-resident Pacific Islanders, Chinese, Hispanic, African, and Native Americans,

(a) by voluntary divestiture. Prior to any voluntary sale of controlling interest in a company in an industry that has been certified as socially overconcentrated or socially monopolized, the sellers will notify the Department of Justice and the Department of Commerce, of the proposed sale, and allow forty-five days for the presentation of bids by indigenous minority purchasers. Government grants, loans, and loan guarantees will be used to facilitate the acquisition.

In examining the structure of markets, and the degree of concentration, the government shall include as a consideration the participation of Pacific Islanders, Hispanic, Chinese, African, and Native Americans. The government will act to encourage, through the application of this Act, the increased participation of these groups in industrial and commercial activity as owners and investors.

Definitions

Social monopoly—A market condition in which indigenous Pacific Islanders, Hispanic-, Chinese-, African-, and Native American firms, in the aggregate, account for less than 5 percent of aggregate sales, or less than 5 percent of assets, whichever is smaller.

Social overconcentration—A market condition in which any race, in the aggregate, controls more than 95 percent of the aggregate sales of an industry, or more than 95 percent of the assets, whichever is greater.

IS THIS PROPOSAL REALISTIC?

Let's be realistic. This kind of legislation is a very long shot. It is based on a theory that would take decades to become acceptable. Back in the early 1970s, however, Senator Philip Hart of Michigan was chairman of the Subcommittee on Monopoly and Antitrust of the Senate Judiciary Subcommittee. In the 1950s that subcommittee had been Senator Estes Kefauver's platform for innovative investigations. Later, it was chaired by Senator Edward Kennedy (D–Mass.). This subcommittee has historically been chaired by activists who have used it to ask important social rather than merely narrow technical questions. Considering this tradition, at some point it might seriously take up an avant garde idea like racial social monopoly. In fact, Senator Hart did have a similar idea in his proposal, which he called the Industrial Reorganization Act. This act called for divestiture of powerful concentrations in the interest of efficiency. At the same time, Senator Hart was also determined to do something about inequity and dangerous power concentrations.

During a recess in the hearing on his proposed act in the early 1970s, Hart, when asked about his Industrial Reorganization Act, stated that he judged it to be so controversial that he thought it stood only a slim chance of getting out of committee, let alone being passed by the full Senate. Thus, he decided to delete a concept in the act akin to the racial monopoly provision, for he concluded that it would add more controversy and hopelessly doom the bill. Such a concept remains controversial today. Nevertheless, it could help solve our present economic problems of lagging output and inefficiency, and contribute to social participation and vigor. The subsidies needed to help indigenous racial minority owners acquire banks and businesses would be payments on the social debt.

5

Narrow Inequalities in Income and Wealth

A decent provisioning for the poor is the true test of civilization.
— Samuel Johnson

It's better to be rich and healthy than poor and sick.
— Ronald Reagan

When will we get paid for the work we have already done?
— Jesse Jackson

Maldistribution becomes a practical problem for everyone when the victims realize how badly they are being treated. Awareness of the magnitude, rather than mere awareness of the fact of injustice, is more likely to stimulate correction. Information about injustice is the key to ending or severely reducing it. Today we have more powerful information on injustice than ever before, and things will never be the same.

POVERTY AND DISPARITIES

In 1990, a total of 36 million Americans were classified as below poverty level. By counting noncash benefits, however, the total can be reduced to about 23 million. Conservatives generally want to count those benefits because it suggests that things aren't really so bad and that not much more direct intervention is needed or justified. Liberals, on the other hand, generally argue that the key number is earned income, which means that these millions of Americans cannot participate fully. Therefore, we need to do more to help them become competitive so that they can earn their way.

In 1990, 12.6 percent of black married couples were in poverty, compared to only 5.4 percent of white married couples.[1] We can pick any data point in the period to get the picture. For example, by 1984, in an economy that was seemingly performing well, officially 15 percent of Americans were in poverty (then defined as four-person households with cash income under $10,178). However, when noncash benefits were added, only 9.6 percent were in poverty. Those relationships have held more or less unchanged for two decades. By 1992 the picture remained the same.

Some of those classified as "poor" are only temporarily down on their luck; others are poorer than before because they have retired; and still others are in school preparing to become affluent. Perhaps 40 percent of the poor are hard core. Since many of these are young, female-headed households, breaking the teenage parent patterns may help reduce poverty. (We focus on this important issue in chapter 8.)

We spend $80 billion on means-tested benefits, including AFDC, Medicaid, food stamps, rent subsidies, and some Social Security. If the $80 billion went to the hard-core poor only in transfer payments, most would be out of poverty, but they would still be dependent. Making them productive—transferring capital, training, tools, housing, and equity to them—is key. In the 1992 primary campaign, Paul Tsongas correctly emphasized market-based rather than public sector redistributive strategies. That is how most jobs will be created, and full employment, especially in distressed communities, can be reached and sustained.

As noted earlier, if we include food stamps, health, housing, and noncash subsidies, the number of families in poverty is reduced by 20 to 40 percent. However, here we are concerned with the powerful impact of earned income on morale and economic performance. Continually subsidizing people who feel cheated is not the way to help them become full participants. Nor does it help to pay the social debt.

In the 1980s, 8 million, or 60 percent, of the 14 million families in poverty received in-kind or noncash benefits. Forty percent of them got food stamps, 40 percent Medicaid, 24 percent subsidized housing, and 65 percent school lunches. The challenge is to help these people earn their way and changing the distribution of earned income is one way to promote this goal. Pointing to the income supplement programs, as many people do, avoids the issue that opportunities to work, save, invest, and compete are unfairly restricted. That is where the serious disparities are.

Of all African-American households, 25 percent got food stamps, 50 percent school lunches, 25 percent subsidized housing, and 33 percent Medicaid. However, these programs do not really appear to enrich the poor. Of the 14.3 million households in poverty, 8.0 million got one benefit, 3.7 million two benefits, 2 million three benefits, and 0.46 million four benefits. Economists Sheldon Danzinger, Robert Haveman, and Robert Plotnick, after reviewing many studies on income transfers, found that, depending on how you look at it, transfers increased the bottom 20 percent's income share from 5.69 percent of income to 9.9 percent. Economists argue over which transfers to count and how to count them, but that misses the point. Increasing earnings should be the goal.

The guaranteed annual income, or the negative income tax, would give everyone who needed it and qualified on an objective income test the cash transfers required to rise above poverty. Although they would replace in-kind programs, they, too, would tend to perpetuate dependency. They also avoid the issue of restitution.

BLACK POVERTY FLUCTUATES BUT PERSISTS

In 1966, 42 percent of black people were in poverty; by 1969, after the Great Society had been launched, it was down to 32 percent. By 1981, however, it had risen to 34 percent, remaining in that range in 1990. When the Reagan administration cut budgets for social programs and altered tax rules in the 1980s, it shifted income to the top 20 percent. Households under $11,500 gave up $7.2 billion. Households over $47,800 received $38 billion. The cut in the top marginal tax rate, from 70 to 50 percent, achieved much of this reverse redistribution. These kinds of policies essentially continued through 1990. By 1991 the economy was stalling dangerously, and one major reason was the persistence of equity and distributional problems.

Some economists claim that little income inequality, by race or otherwise, exists because the usual measures fail to consider that households have different-aged heads and breadwinners. Even when distributions are adjusted in this way, significant income inequality still remains. The bottom 20 percent receives 8 percent instead of only 5 percent. Other economists counter that we should adjust for double earners, husband and wife, for then the distribution would show how much effort is needed to generate each share of income. It takes more effort to earn a higher family income than it used to.

There are yet other ways to criticize what the income distributions seem to tell us. Thus, all the technical adjustments necessary should be made to ensure true comparability. When all is said and done, however, there is still a gross discrepancy of earned income, adjusted for any social characteristics anyone cares to emphasize.

Of course, we do tend to distort the true picture. For example, the age of the people behind those numbers is not considered. Critics have a point here. Retired homeowners who own free and clear, or low-income medical students who look forward to very high incomes, for example, are not "poor" in the same sense as other people with the same reported income. Even when such factors are accounted for, however, we still do not have a fair distribution. Moreover, it is doubtful whether natural processes will lead to one, despite the stimulus of general tax cuts, investment incentives, and reduced regulation. It all boils down to the following relationship: white median income is $36,000, and black median income is $22,000. White median wealth is $44,000, and black median wealth is $4,000.[2]

WHAT SHOULD THE DISTRIBUTION BE?

The actual distribution fluctuates around these relationships.

Bottom 20	5%
Next	12
Middle	17
Next	24
Top	42

But a fair distribution might look like this.

Bottom 20	10%
Next	15
Middle	20
Next	25
Top	30

A "fair" distribution might be approached by, say, 2020. The point is not simply a top to bottom ratio of 3 to 1; rather, the objective is earned income at that ratio. No doubt, a fair distribution can be depicted in many ways, some of which are more radical than others. Clearly, however, the existing distribution is based on historic injustice and is neither fair nor healthy.

WEALTH DISTRIBUTIONS

Wealth, like income, is also maldistributed. In this regard, the racial disparity is dramatic. In 1988 white household net worth was $43,279 and black net worth was $4,169.[3] The processes that produce income gaps also produce gaps in wealth. The top 0.5 percent of households hold 35 percent of wealth, over $11 trillion, and the top 10 percent hold 70 percent. The top 0.5 percent, 420,000 households, averaged $8.8 million in net worth, the next 0.5 percent averaged $1.7 million; and the next 9 percent $420,000. Everyone else, the next 80 percent, averaged $40,000. These Joint Economic Committee figures can be criticized. Although there are probably errors based on small sample and other problems, the basic relationships, the overconcentration, and the reality of how wealth is accumulated are beyond dispute.

If we examine all wealth in terms of the social debt, we get another interesting perspective. Roughly, we have

$ 10 trillion = real personal net worth

   10 trillion = institutional and public worth

   25 trillion = the present value of the labor force of over 100 million people

With 80 percent of the labor force white, $20 trillion represents the present value of its projected lifetime earnings stream. Now, $1 to $2 trillion, or 5 to 10 percent of that total, represents benefits that can be attributed to training and education obtained through past racial discrimination in their favor. At a minimum, then, the social debt, in terms of wealth, might be on the order of $1.5 to $3 trillion. Rather than focus on these mind-boggling numbers, we should use another way to look at the current consequences of past unjust relationships. Both these disparities and their manner of creation reinforce the need for restitution.

THE FORBES 400

Every year, *Forbes* magazine lists the 400 wealthiest individuals—those with a minimum net worth of $150 million—and the 82 wealthiest families —those with a minimum net worth of $200 million. In most years, over 90 percent of the families and 60 to 70 percent of the 400 individuals inherited their wealth. One year, the combined net worth of the 482 individuals and families was $166 billion in business investments. It is leveraged so that they control much of the institutional power in society. Thus, these families can control over $2,000 billion in assets—40 percent of all fixed business capital. This wealth is power. It is too concentrated, however, and it can be traced, in part, to economic injustice.

FAIRNESS AND PRODUCTIVITY

We have looked at earned income and wealth distributions, adjustments for government programs, racial comparisons, disagreements over interpretations, and proposed "ideal" distributions in the future. We have also considered that the earned income and wealth distributions are distorted by injustice. Improved information will raise public awareness of how income and wealth are maldistributed, and that will stimulate the political resolve to correct the distribution in ways that are therapeutic for economic performance. If the bottom 20 can increase its share and *earn* 10 percent of total income, it will mean that redistributive and training programs have put them in a better relative competitive position. That will reflect a healthier, fairer society, and it will mean that all people are producing and contributing.

TRICKLE DOWN?

Many voters apparently want to keep the earned distribution as it is. They claim to be concerned about investment incentives. They fear that progressive taxation and redistribution will harm incentives for the top 20. Therefore, they prefer to stress capital gains tax cuts as the way to generate a broad economic thrust and job creation. Theirs is a legitimate concern. Redistributing income and wealth should be done in a way that rewards effort and investor risk-taking. Punitive and confiscatory redistribution is not the idea. Due process, rigorous analysis, and free and open debate are required, ensuring that the top 20 percent does not withdraw, sulk, and feel put upon, as it has in England and Sweden. But trickle-down solutions do not really work, tending instead to further distort income and wealth shares. In addition, the kinds of tax formulas that are offered as necessary incentives for investment and creativity are usually overly generous, unnecessary, and subject to manipulation by "paper entrepreneurs."[4]

By 2020, through conscious policy, the top 20 could be limited to 30 percent of all earned income, and the bottom 20 could be raised to 10 percent. Sensible policies can achieve that goal. Far from being a utopian scheme, this is a realistic target, representing a substantial improvement. Although it does not eliminate poverty (can poverty ever be completely vanquished?), it does reduce gross differences. It is not drastic, and it would not damage incentives to invent, invest, develop, and do aggressive business.

It is also desirable to provide more effective incentives to wage earners and to the have nots. Incentive problems exist at all levels, not just for investors. The objective is not equal but fair shares. The 2020 shares should closely reflect everyone's true economic contribution. A top-to-bottom ratio of 3 to 1 for 2020 is closer than the current ratio of over 8 to 1 to what we would normally expect when everyone has a fair chance to contribute and be rewarded.

THE PROTESTANT ETHIC

Now suppose that miraculously all wealth and income were handed out again to everyone in equal amounts. In a couple of generations, some people would again control far larger shares of wealth and income than others. In fact, it is argued, after a while, the income distribution would look about the way it does today! The top 20 would again emerge to receive eight times as much as the bottom 20. Some find this picture comforting, for it justifies the current distribution as natural.

Discrimination and exclusion from opportunities for education, training, hiring, and capital for business development are not significant reasons for tolerating disparities from top to bottom or between races. The distribution will return to this "normal" pattern because the most able people will always work harder and do better. They will plan, organize, save, and invest better, and consequently will live smarter. Therefore, they will end up on top again because they are sharper and more virtuous.

Obviously, this assessment contains some truth. Talent is not equally given within major racial and ethnic groups. But the real issue is this: Would the present income and wealth distributions hold had there been open and fair competition over the last fifteen generations, or even the last five generations? The answer is, "no." The distributions and shares would now look more like the "ideal" goal of 2020, and that's where public policies should head. There would still be poverty but not to the degree seen today. What is more, the have nots would not be disproportionately African American. The desired distribution can become a government priority. Trickle down does not work, but restitution theory can establish that redistributive policies will clearly be fair.

6

Affirmative Action, Competitiveness, and Productivity

I accept that in the social sciences, some things are better not said.
—Daniel P. Moynihan

Generally, public policy analysts, politicians, journalists, bureaucrats, corporate managers, and everyday citizens initially object to restitution theory. Many also object to affirmative action, as was illustrated, for example, in the 1991 debate over the civil rights bill and in the David Duke guberatorial campaign in Louisiana. The reasons are similar. Affirmative action is redistributive, but redistribution is vital to restoring justice and equity, and hence, efficiency, productivity, and competitiveness. The question is, not whether but how do we redistribute. Effective management requires a solid rationale that generates broad support.

AFFIRMATIVE ACTION'S THREE LEVELS

Bradford Reynolds, the Reagan administration's assistant attorney general for civil rights, fought many forms of affirmative action. His reason was that "Affirmative Action means making an outreach effort to minorities and women to apply for jobs. It doesn't mean granting race or sex conscious jobs to the less qualified." That definition of affirmative action—stop formal discrimination, improve educational opportunities, and make sure everyone knows there are entry-level opportunities by recruiting and advertising widely—is the conservative strict constructionist approach. It is level 1 affirmative action.

Level 2 affirmative action would have schools, employers, and government agencies go further and distribute some benefits—employment entry, admissions, contracts, and scholarships—to minorities on some preferential basis for a limited time.

Level 3 is the most liberal. It would use timetables and goals (what level 1 critics would label "quotas") to target benefits in an explicitly redistributive way. Discussion of affirmative action has been confused in part because these distinctions have not been clearly labeled. Moreover, the points of view have blurred.

AFFIRMATIVE ACTION REDISTRIBUTES INCOME

Allocational issues tend to be divisive and emotionally charged. Suggestions that the have nots should receive more of a static economic pie and the haves somewhat less, for any reason, provokes a reaction.

Affirmative action has aroused hostility from the start, partly because it is perceived as inherently redistributive. Although level 3 is the most sensitive, many haves and middles tend to see even less progressive forms as unfair. Affirmative action reallocates scarce and maldistributed resources and opportunities. Level 3, if properly designed and managed, could provide a way to pay some of the social debt.

Based simply on demographics, some private and public policies give preference to qualified Hispanic, Native, or African-American applicants over equal competitors for jobs, training, scholarships, mortgage money, business loans, small business service, construction, and supply contracts, and openings in medical, business, engineering, and law schools. This is level 2. This arrangement rankles many people, for it seems unfair. Level 3 goes even farther. Where is the justification?, it is asked. Should schools, government agencies, and employers do anything to change their demographics? Is there any reason to change the way opportunities are distributed? Should the relative distributions of income and wealth be changed? And if so, how extensive should the proactive policies be, level 2 or level 3?

By 1990 the economy had become burdened in ways that will cause continuing problems through the decade. Policies in the 1980s produced unanticipated negative consequences. Stagnation and decline are hard to reverse when traditional expansionary policy options are constrained by large budget deficits and by a work force damaged by persistent underinvestment in education and training. The total economic pie will likely not grow as rapidly as it did from the 1960s through the 1980s, despite, or perhaps because of, supply side policies. If improved overall performance is desired, however, the United States has to improve economic conditions for the have nots and help them become productive.

Since disproportionate numbers of African Americans are have nots, even level 1 affirmative action will give them more tools and training to participate in the economy productively. But there's a dilemma. With little or no real economic growth taking place, where do the resources needed to pay for upgrading their skills come from? The only possibility is to take resources from the haves. In the absence of enough growth, redistribution must take place; otherwise there will be little improvement for the have nots at the bottom. Redistribution of wealth and income has little appeal, however. It is seen as unfair. Since, as many believe, we've earned what we have, government should not tax any away to spend on, invest in, or give to others, except those in dire straits—the truly disadvantaged,[1] the deserving poor.[2]

Affirmative action, especially levels 2 and 3, often seems a zero sum game. Yet no one has ever clearly explained what the problem is and how those forms of proactive affirmative action are solutions. Nor has the means to strengthen the economy ever been explained. Instead, they have been presented as civil rights and social engineering issues.

THE DOWNSIDE

As Shelby Steele[3] and Stephen Carter[4] emphasize, another problem is that level 3, level 2, and even level 1 can produce unanticipated negative consequences for many intended beneficiaries. Professionals, students, and employees, as well as small business owners, however good they might be, when perceived as undeserving or uncompetitive, can be stigmatized. Many may even become uneasy about their own worth. Admissions, procurement, lending, hiring, and promotion policies—level 1—can all ensure that these new entrants get opportunities to train, enter, and compete, opportunities that were previously denied to people like them. Then once in, it is assumed that they will work hard. It is also assumed that they will mature. Then, at the end of training, they are expected to be competitive with all others admitted by "normal" processes. Their subsequent careers and business ventures are expected to be of the same quality as everyone else's. They may have been slightly behind when admitted to college or professional or graduate school, or to a training program, or into business with a subsidy of some kind. That is not supposed to be a perpetual problem, however. The gap is presumed to close while they are there. Then, once they are launched and are going up the learning curve, in careers or in business, their performance is expected, on average, to be comparable with that of all others.

We do not yet know enough about testing for admissions. Specifically, we do not have exact knowledge of what qualities in candidates for admission will ultimately lead to success in business, medicine, law, or engineering. Thus, the meaning of "qualified" is not as obvious as most critics of affirmative action would have us believe. It turns out that much of the debate is based on ignorance. We need to know more about screening and selection and about what personal characteristics matter. Nevertheless, experience shows that affirmative action, especially levels 2 and 3, can create problems. Affirmative action at these levels seems to disregard conventional processes in ways that seem unfair to other candidates who narrowly miss admission, as in the *Bakke* case, or to those whose business doesn't get the contract, or to those who aren't promoted to middle or senior management as soon as they had hoped.

AFFIRMATIVE ACTION IN EMPLOYMENT AND EDUCATION

Presumably, we want to see everyone perform at optimum levels in all occupations as quickly as possible so that the economy will work well. How quickly can we effectively achieve that goal? Level 1 affirmative action can help people enter previously exclusionary occupations very quickly, almost immediately. Then levels 2 and 3 have been used to accelerate promotions, and candidates have been promoted over people with long tenure. The result can be damaging to organizational harmony.

Entry-level recruitment (level 1) seems to work reasonably well; well-managed, rationally explained, accelerated upward mobility (level 2) can, too. The greatest resistance seems to occur when promotions and mid- and senior-level recruiting (level 3) seems to be at the direct expense of people who have patiently waited their turn or feel financially insecure.

What about level 3? Is it desirable to use affirmative action to rush less experienced people into middle and senior jobs or into business contract opportunities? Is it OK to set aside jobs, contracts, or capital for people whose test scores or seniority are not as high as those of others? That is where antagonisms, controversy, and lack of clear consensus seem the greatest. In some cases it has been too dramatic. Therefore, level 2 may be more likely to generate fewer unanticipated negative consequences. Improved quality of applicants for most jobs and educational slots will ultimately be based on improvements in early family life and on better preschool and kindergarten preparation. Level 1 can be justified and sustained for forty to sixty years, whereas levels 2 and 3 may have to have "sunsets" of no more than forty years.

Thus, with a level 2 approach, racial near-parity in medical, business, engineering, and law school admissions, as well as in management and business and in many skilled occupations would be more gradual than some civil rights level 3 advocates would prefer. In ten or twenty years, however, because of sharp improvements at early educational levels, and in the social environment, applicants for advanced and professional training and for business development and financing will be truly competitive. They will then be able to compete and contribute in schools, industrial training programs, and business. In the meantime, in some cases accelerating the process unduly (level 3) has produced students and graduates with marginal self-confidence and performance.

Affirmative action should not artificially bring people into business, professional schools, or technical employment who are not ready. Of course, the words "are not ready" are red flag words. They have been used by intransigents and hard-line exclusionists for a long time. Now, however, we can progress rapidly, admitting people who are ready to compete even though their "scores" might not be as high as those of others. Although the pool of "qualified" applicants is limited, natural processes will fill the pool with qualified competitive people.

By now most decision makers are acting in good faith and will not exclude racially. Hence, a moderate compromise, level 2, can be pursued widely; it assumes increased good faith. Affirmative action is also intended to overcome the resistance of many lending, purchasing, admissions, and hiring officers who have been hostile and untrustworthy. Their natural preferences were exclusionary, destructive, and unjust.

Most managers see themselves as middle or upper middle-class haves, and they regard level 2 and 3 affirmative action as redistributing benefits from them to people who have not earned them. They therefore are ambivalent about or want to sabotage those policies. For this reason, in the 1960s it was necessary to preserve affirmative action in lending and contracting, admissions, and hiring in order to overcome their resistance. Today we witness more genuine good faith and decent efforts.

As long as we continue to see steady evidence, we can trust that level 2 will work. Let decision makers treat applicants fairly, and in ten or twenty years, natural processes will produce fair and effective outcomes. After that, there will be reasonable levels of participation in occupations, employment, advanced education, and business, and less need for as much level 3 affirmative action. In any case, the objective is not strict representation according to population proportion, for that would be artificial, inefficient, and contrary to our tendencies to concentrate in certain occupations and businesses by ethnic group.

John Bunzel, formerly of the U.S. Civil Rights Commission, speaks for many when he says, "Some people would have us believe it is fair and just to discriminate against white people to make up for the wrongs committed by previous generations against black Americans." Bunzel sets up a common strawman. Hardly anyone advocates that kind of "reverse discrimination."[5] His simplifications and distortions seem deliberate. Affirmative action seeks to fairly change distributions of income, wealth, and opportunities. The rationale most commonly offered is that it will help compensate for past offenses, but that is not the best way to phrase it.

Affirmative action should be advocated as a way to help the economy breathe normally, curing the nation of the chronic bronchitis of economic injustice through racial exclusion. Affirmative redistribution should also be part of the justification for paying restitution. And affirmative action should concentrate on policies to increase the number of good candidates in the pool for openings in schools and jobs, contracts, loans, grants, licenses, and business opportunities. This approach will increase competition, which is good for the economy.

BENIGN NEGLECT AND ECONOMIC RENEWAL

In 1969 Daniel Patrick Moynihan, then an assistant to President Nixon, wrote a private memo to the president on "benign neglect." This neglect referred not so much to African Americans but to public discussion of race. His primary desire was to tone down executive branch and media rhetoric, which had gotten heated and he felt that the president could constructively lead that deescalation. The memorandum was leaked and caused a sensation because it was widely believed to show personal and official hostility. It was also thought to reflect Moynihan's desire to retaliate against critics of his earlier work on the Negro family. In the 1970s and 1980s, however, a growing attitude of policy indifference, if not hostility, began to appear among policy makers and commentators.

Restitution theory establishes the principle that addressing these issues is an obligation rather than a matter of discretion. It cannot, in good faith, be neglected, benignly or otherwise. In the final analysis, however, restitution depends on broad goodwill. The question is, does it exist? In Plato's *Republic*, Cephalus says that Justice is paying one's debts. But Thrasymachus is more tough-minded. He believes that "Justice is the interest of the stronger." Is benign neglect of restitution in the haves' interest? Can they refuse to acknowledge it without damaging the economy's ethical foundations? Is affirmative action, at some proactive level, an option that can be rejected in good conscience?

CHARITY, GENEROSITY, AND GRATITUDE

Public policy toward the have nots is often expressed in terms of charity. Policy makers and other influential people who are haves, look on these basic economic defects in terms of voluntary compassion. Indeed, politicians like to talk about social policy as a matter of compassion; that was the basis for George Bush's "Thousand Points of Light."[6] Therefore, affirmative action gets caught in that pattern of thinking, and gratitude is expected in return. However, the problems of social and economic underperformance stem from major structural defects and past and present injustices, and not simply from a lack of communitarian responsibility to our neighbors.[7] We are not simply our brother's keeper; we are sometimes our brother's debtor. Poverty and chronic dysfunction are not sideline issues, and gratitude is not relevant.

Not long after the Moynihan incident, Vice President Spiro Agnew remarked that African Americans and their leaders were ungrateful for the government's actions on their behalf. But why, one may ask, should gratitude be expressed if a debt is merely being paid? If affirmative action and redistributive policy are ways to correct injustice, gratitude is irrelevant. James Reston had been talking to Agnew: "People," he said, "had forgotten the obligations of charity. Well-heeled people in this country weren't giving more than 10 percent of what they could to the poor, while the poor were accepting handouts from the State without the slightest feeling of *gratitude*."[8] Reston's remarks indicate that the haves want to keep what they have and, at the same time, feel good about themselves. They want expressions of gratitude for their generosity. But neither generosity nor "compassion" is germane to the public policy debate on poverty and inequity. A generous public spirit is important in a civilized social order, or course, and charity, in the biblical sense (love thy neighbor) is an important social value. We should cherish and cultivate this value. However, "generosity" does not help us think clearly about public policy toward economic inequities and remedies like affirmative action. The term implies fiscal charity. However, the have nots do not need charity. They need the capital that is rightfully theirs in the first place, returned to them.

Generosity and charity are hardly the prescription for unemployment and poverty and for revival of the economy. Even great liberals such as former New York Mayor John Lindsay slip into this common form. "I have sometimes wondered, if Brownsville were in Burma, whether our national government would not have responded far faster and with greater *generosity* than it has, so far, here at home." Lindsay understood cities but did not think in terms of restitution. Therefore, the concept of generosity distorted his perspective on how to generate sustained economic revival. Benign neglect, charity, generosity, and gratitude—all these perspectives merely confuse the issue.[9]

SHOCKLEY, INTELLIGENCE, AND RACIAL PARITY

Some observers, both racists and respectable journalists and social scientists, state that fundamental biological deficiencies in intelligence among different races and ethnicities are more important factors in income disparities than injustice. What if education and job opportunities and capital subsidies can never be enough to equip the have nots to produce and contribute? What if black people, on average, can never be as productive as white people in most employment, business, and classroom situations? If that were true, what would be the purpose of affirmative action, no matter how large the social debt?

The idea that intelligence may be based fundamentally in heredity has its supporters. William Shockley's views were summarized by Richard Herrnstein in the 1970s,[10] when this issue again flared up as it does periodically. After examining the Army's preinduction mental tests, Shockley said that he found the IQ of black Americans to be fifteen points lower than that of white Americans. Are those tests valid? That question has long been debated. The charge against IQ tests is as follow: They were designed by and for white middle-class Americans, and, as such, they make no allowance for the cultural, economic, nutritional, and emotional deprivation experienced by many have nots. Nevertheless, Shockley related the results of Army IQ testing to research in Africa by the geneticist T. E. Reed. According to Shockley, Reed found that certain genes found primarily in whites, are found in only limited amounts of less than 1 percent in Africans and that these genes show up more frequently in the blood tests of African Americans. In rural Georgia, it was 11 percent, and in Oakland, California, 22 percent. Questions about the authenticity of Reed's research began to be raised, however.

Shockley apparently wanted to prove that intelligence is in direct proportion to the amount of these distinctive white genes. For each additional 1 percent of these Caucasian genes, he said, the average IQ increased by about one IQ point. He believed that through mixed breeding over the centuries, the IQs of many black Americans might match or somehow exceed those of many white Americans at 30 or 40 percent. The average level of these genes in the white population, he claimed, was 43 percent, a figure indicating that many whites are also deficient in these genes.

Restitution theory views any disparities in IQ between the races as resulting primarily from entrenched injustice. In contrast, Shockley and his like-minded peers feel the problem actually reflects differences in genetic potential for developing the skills and capacities needed in modern society. Whatever the case, some economic disparities are becoming worse with each generation. Shockley believed that welfare promotes dysgenics. The human race, he said, is diminished when genetically disadvantaged, low-quality people reproduce in high numbers. While he believed that this probably occurs in all races, he felt it was more severe in some than in others. He estimated that black Americans had lost five IQ points relative to white Americans since 1918 because there had been less miscegenation in the twentieth century than in the nineteenth and there had accordingly been a progressive reduction in the presence of this particular Caucasian gene.

As a solution, Shockley proposed the payment of federal cash bonuses to intellectually substandard people who agreed not to have children. He also wanted to institute special educational and social programs for substandard people of all groups. Perhaps, to some, such an approach might represent a kind of affirmative action.

MOYNIHAN AND COLEMAN

As mentioned earlier, Daniel P. Moynihan, as assistant secretary of labor from 1963 to 1965, had written a paper on the Negro family in which he concludes that African Americans had evolved a matriarchal family. He felt that this pattern was seriously out of line with the rest of society, putting black people at a serious disadvantage in a generally patriarchal culture.

At about the same time, James S. Coleman's research, authorized by the 1964 Civil Rights Act, sought to determine inequities in public schools. The study found that African Americans lagged in achievement at every grade level, one through twelve. What is more, the differences increased with age. Some blamed underbudgeted segregated schools for that difference. But the study did not find that school quality had any clear effect on achievement among white children. If the schools themselves caused the poor performance, all poor schools could be expected to have that effect. Thus, many analysts began to think that perhaps the difference lay in the black children's cultural surroundings at home rather than in the quality of their schools. Both Moynihan and Coleman, then, suggested that something in Afro America had retarded its economic and educational progress. Although they did not deny the clear evidence that customs and laws also contributed to the lag, both said that removing external barriers did not always bring improvement. The implication was that there were internal problems within the family or culture.

Moynihan and Department of Health, Education and Welfare Secretary John Gardner, commenting on Coleman's study blamed cultural history and slavery. Berkeley's Arthur R. Jensen, however, said that the problem could be attributed to differences in inherited intelligence.

Let us for the moment set aside technical questions on the interpretation and validity of IQ tests. Even if we accept the tests as useful, neither Shockley, Jensen, Moynihan, Coleman, Herrnstein nor any other investigator has presented a suitable sample of African Americans who have enjoyed, along with their ancestors, a proper investment in their education and training, including on-the-job training, over several generations. That is because they were victims of economic injustice whereby educational capital was deliberately and coercively diverted from them to others— thus contributing to the social debt and undermining their ability to participate fully in the economy.

High intelligence may correlate with high-status occupations and with high income and wealth, but to people like Shockley and Jensen, high income and wealth, in the aggregate, also have strong social and biological associations. Would the apparent relationships among race, intelligence, and income persist if investment in education had been historically appropriate and just, that is, roughly equal across society? That seems unlikely. There has been a serious underinvestment in educating the have nots. Indeed, through discrimination in budgets, the have nots of all races have subsidized the education of the haves for several generations.

If it were possible to get agreement on intelligence tests, finding systematic, significant differences in intelligence might be feasible. Let us allow that possibility for a moment, and, to exhaust all possibilities, let us further assume that we might even find that, on economic grounds, equal expenditures per pupil are not justified, simply because some people are fundamentally unable to benefit from the investment in their education. They are incapable of giving society a reasonable return on that investment. The trouble with that assumption is that political decision processes have diverted education resources from African Americans to benefit other Americans. African Americans have had little or no say in those educational budget decisions.

None of these controversial investigations can answer the question of what the 1990s would have shown if there been equal expenditures per pupil over, say, the last six generations. This is why the kind of case that came to the Supreme Court in 1991, changing Mississippi's funding of separate race colleges, misses the point.[11] Blacks were wrongfully coerced into subsidizing the higher education of whites. Therefore, money is owed, and it should be paid in the form of massive investments in Jackson State University, Alcorn, and so on.

With historically equal investments in education and training, the races, for practical purposes, would be close to equal today. If capital is redistributed through educational budgeting, it can reasonably be concluded that people can contribute fully to the economy. To make the investment really pay off, however, adequate funding of other important related items like housing and health is also needed. The argument about heredity—genetics and racial intelligence and resulting status—is not relevant. Past discrimination in educational financing has led to the accumulation of a social debt, and so it is that investment in education is owed. That will improve the work force as well as aggregate performance. At issue here is not compensatory education but compensation itself. Much of it should be for education, however.

While these controversies continue, the idea of restitution never entered the discussion. Redistributive justice would ultimately benefit everyone, but obviously the best time to consider affirmative action is when the economy is expanding, with employment full and people confident of the future and outward looking. All in all, however, redistributive remedies will have slim support if tight economic conditions hold. In the presence of prolonged economic sluggishness and personal fear, people will naturally resist affirmative action.

RESENTMENT AGAINST AFFIRMATIVE ACTION

No matter what the prevailing conditions may be, restitution theory produces resentment. "It's time blacks began to moderate their demands," Nathan Glazer says. Believing that African-American demands are excessive and impinge on the rights of others, he suggests that we get "clear on what we owe each other, what we owe ourselves, and what we owe the nation as a whole." He wants us to avoid thinking we owe each other more than we do, and he especially wants an end to "self-flagellation." Generally, he states, we all concur that we owe each other "nondiscrimination, equal opportunity in education and employment, equality before the courts, political power roughly proportionate to the number of each group."[12]

Many efforts have indeed been made to ensure social equity and efficiency. Demands have been put forward by aggrieved groups and then sustained, modified, or withdrawn. This give-and-take continues. People and groups who make demands, or even requests, frequently have to modify them because their perceived needs and their strength and bargaining situations change. Sometimes they recognize that the original demands were poorly articulated or technically deficient or sometimes even unfair or outrageous. But restitution theory clarifies "what we owe each other." Glazer's list of what we owe can be extended to include the most common debt: he forgot to mention money.

Others who have also been discriminated against—by gender, ethnicity, religion—feel treating racial discrimination as a priority is itself unjust. Caution must be shown not to create a sense of competition among aggrieved classes.

Affirmative action should be regarded as a major step toward correcting economic injustice, making restitution, paying the social debt, and promoting efficiency and renewal. However, that does not preclude justice for other have nots. It simply recognizes that the size, scope, scale, duration, and impact of this particular injustice makes it worthwhile to give it some priority. Nonetheless, the debate on affirmative action continues to generate passionate resentment and hostility. That is because other have nots have too often felt that their grievances have been ignored and their case belittled. Restitution theory can help everyone understand the full significance of the injustices and their relative impact on overall social performance, and it can give some sense of priority in deciding remedies.

THE BAKKE CASE

In the late 1970s, Allen Bakke, a white applicant sued the University of California at Davis, charging that its affirmative action admissions policies constituted discrimination against whites. Although an able student, the university had rejected his application for admission to the medical school. The university contended that its admissions policies were designed, among other things, to help remedy the effects of past discrimination or to rectify past neglect, as the press commonly put it. But that is not the best way to look at it. Some observers believe that Bakke was being discriminated against by the school to make make up for wrongs that he had no part in or to redress past discrimination. Even Harvard's Archibald Cox, arguing the University of California's case before the Court, put it that way. Justice Potter Stewart asked whether Davis's procedure "put a limit on the number of white people?" Cox replied, "Yes, but the program is in the public interest, nonetheless. It undoes generations of racial discrimination, produces classroom diversity, supplies Afro, Hispanic, and other nonwhite professionals, breaks down isolation and exclusion, and provides role models for younger people."

While interesting reasons, they are not the most critical ones, nor do they go to the heart of the issue as other resentful outsiders have seen it. If race is to be a factor in admissions policy, the strongest reason is that each spot in a university represents a public investment in human capital. That is, each spot represents money. Since money is owed, efforts to find and admit the well qualified—affirmative action—is a way to pay off that debt. Rather than remedying past discrimination or rectification, the primary goal should be to pay a current social debt that will help produce a society that is unburdened by a corrosive injustice, and that benefits from the full contribution of every member. Providing greater opportunities for professional education is one way, although a sunset point should be set, say, forty more years. After this point, the remedy will have been completed. Past exclusionary racial discrimination in admissions to professional schools unfairly continues to benefit most members and potential members of those professions as a class. Therefore, a redistributive remedy should include affirmative action in recruiting candidates for admission to graduate and professional schools.

One might well counter that many people descended from European immigrants also suffered discrimination. Indeed, their direct ancestors were victims of the same or similar process themselves in Europe or here, as Krauthammer noted. How, then, are they beneficiaries of this particular form of economic injustice—racial discrimination? Although individual beneficiaries cannot be identified, if their income and wealth put them in the top 30 percent, they are the haves and they can be presumed to benefit. Historically, despite their ethnicity, they were usually allowed to move into the queue. Their race allowed them to displace potential black candidates, as Hershberg found. But ethnic discrimination may also deserve a redistributive policy remedy if it produces a social debt.

NOBLESSE OBLIGE?

Almost every ethnic group, tribe, or nation has, at some time, exploited another group or been exploited in turn. At least, in theory, then, debts are owed all around. Giving any one group priority attention riles the others, for everyone has known injustice. However, certain distinctions are justified, some injustices, as Bittker noted, can be assigned priority for correction. Therefore, we should not conclude that since everyone has been harmed at some time, no one is entitled to a remedy unless everyone is simultaneously.

Affirmative action has stimulated "reverse discrimination" suits that basically ask why affirmative action is justified for some groups and not for others. Some plaintiffs in reverse discrimination suits state that they recognize the existence of special problems, and they concede that some targeted remedies are justified. It is just that they, too, are part of a class that is entitled to a remedy for injustice. Others, however, deny any differences, even though race is special. We can see how by examining upward mobility in corporate management. Who are the top ten officers in the 2,000 biggest banks and businesses? And who are the 600,000 millionaires and 900,000 highest paid doctors, lawyers, military officers, academics, government officials, entrepreneurs, and executives? A good guess is that 50 percent or more trace their families to low- or middle-income people no more than two generations back. Most have risen to the top 20 from the bottom 30 within two generations. How did they move from relative disadvantage to the upper middle or even lower upper class so quickly? Most did it by hard work, education, training opportunities, luck, perception, and planning. Few of them were geniuses; although they had talent, it was not extraordinary.

Many Hispanic, African, and Native Americans have as much native endowment, but they are not well represented in those top occupational and income categories. Why haven't they risen from have not to have status in two generations? The answer is that systematic economic injustice in the form of racial discrimination has been more potent than other forms of economic injustice. Resentment against affirmative action is normal and human, and should be respected and taken into account. In addition, it matters politically. However, we also need to understand and explain the realities of social justice.

Disadvantaged whites have always been able to rise on merit and luck. Disadvantaged blacks, regardless of talent, have been systematically blocked until the past thirty years. It has always been possible for individual disadvantaged whites in the bottom thirty to make it if they worked hard and got a break. It was never possible for blacks to do that, except for a few truly exceptional entrepreneurs operating in "sheltered markets" with a black customer base. This situation began to change in about 1965, but impediments are still relatively greater, on average, for blacks than for whites, and the benefits from past discrimination, the unjust enrichment, is still a major asset for whites.

Many haves will not be open to the idea of restitution or affirmative action, no matter how it relates to the United States' general economic revitalization. They feel put upon by the pressures and events of the past twenty years. Energy, recession, and other resource-scarcity problems have frightened many into feeling a new sense of vulnerability. Consequently, they are in no mood to think about restitution or affirmative action. With these complex resentments, affirmative action and other remedial policies face formidable negative predispositions.

Paul Seabury, a political scientist at the University of California, has commented on "collective historical injustices": "Most of us . . . can . . . conjure up some collective bestiality, to *our* kind of people, done by *their* kind of people: religious and political persecutions, pogroms, enslavement."[13] Restitution theory resolves the tension generated by such a view, allowing us to see the economic and social justice in affirmative action and to recognize how it relates to economic renewal, productivity, competitiveness, growth, and the general welfare. What does it do for our overall ability to produce, create jobs and income, and build economic security for all? That is how racial injustice should be considered. How can remedies fit the overall management of a country facing complex changes, internally and internationally?

7

Invest in Reducing Crime

The solution to the crime problem will not be found in the social
worker's files, the psychiatrist's notes or the bureaucrat's budget; it
is a problem of the human heart and it is there we must look for
answers.

—Charles Silberman

The United States must restore and maintain its social health both for
its own sake and for utilitarian reasons; that is, it will make the nation
more productive and competitive. A major impediment exists, however.
Adequate education, employment, and economic rewards are impossible
in the presence of fear. Physical fear is broadly felt today, constraining
investors, employers, retailers, customers, and many others. Our present
high crime rates cannot be tolerated indefinitely. The problem of counterproductive criminal behavior must be solved through conventional law
enforcement and innovations in crime prevention, rehabilitation, and
persuasion.

BEHAVE YOURSELF

As a rough estimate, $100 to $200 billion should be paid on the social
debt over the next twenty to forty years in the form of innovative, state-
of-the-art corrections and law enforcement programs. These programs
should aim to change behavior and produce citizen respect for functional
standards of behavior. A package of programs are needed; as shorthand,
they can be labeled "Behave Yourself."

Crime impedes investment, education, housing rehabilitation, job generation, and economic growth and generally stifles renewal. It also

undermines productivity and competitiveness. In order to upgrade the poor and marginal so that they can participate in and contribute to the economy, the crime rate must be cut drastically. People must be reminded to behave; otherwise, everything else we try will simply be waste of effort and resources. Healing chronically ill sectors depends on minimizing crime. Liberal orthodoxy insists that sufficient investment in health, education, training, and housing will create full employment and stable neighborhoods, as well as the conditions that will reduce crime rates. In an ideal world it might work that way, but in the real world of limited resources and political ambivalence, the most likely successful sequence runs the other way. Attack crime directly; then conditions will exist in which investment can occur in housing, education, retailing, and light service and manufacturing businesses. That will create jobs and incomes will rise.

Paying for first-rate law enforcement and crime prevention, including innovative programs using persuasive communications, is an important element in a comprehensive program. And it is one way to help pay the debt.

CRIME IMPEDES DEVELOPMENT

Any data points selected during the past fifteen years—since roughly the end of the Vietnam War—would show the problem of crime to be of the same magnitude. As in the earlier discussions of income and wealth shares, conditions have not changed much in the past fifteen years, though there have been some fluctuations.

Crime has stunted the economic development of the have nots, preventing them from gaining the skills and attitudes they need to enter and succeed in the work force. Administrations can tinker with tax incentives, development subsidies, training, transfer payments, marketing, and management assistance strategies; they can come up with all sorts of partisan and politically expedient "growth packages," and they can fiddle with interest rates and the money supply. But the problems respond only partially and unpredictably. The economy remains relatively lackluster even in periods of recovery and expansion because a chronic injustice has handicapped 20 percent of the population and chronic misbehavior has reinforced the consequences of prior existing conditions. We cannot turn the South Bronx around until better ways are found to help people live conventional, disciplined lives.

In surveys of business location decisions, crime, low-quality labor, poor transportation, and moving costs, in that order, are usually cited as major impediments to moving into proposed enterprise zones in distressed areas. Taxes and zoning are not as critical. "Low-quality labor" is a euphemism for nasty attitudes, a cousin of criminality. Law-abiding conditions can be restored in all neighborhoods. Most have nots do obey the law and behave themselves. As for those who do not, they can be reached, for we have the tools. We can clean up the harassment and uncertainty that contaminates high-crime areas.

WHAT IS TO BE DONE?

The National Center on Institutions and Corrections states that it is possible to identify the 15 percent of young criminals in juvenile facilities who are likely to commit violent crimes, put them in secure facilities, and invest heavily in rehabilitation, support, mentoring, and counseling. That kind of targeting would pay off in successful rehabilitation for many of them and in less harsh penalties for the other 85 percent who do not constitute as great a menace. Many experts believe that personalized, decentralized, community-based techniques work for many.

By 1991, there were 1.1 million inmates in U.S. prisons,[1] twice the 1980 figure and triple the 1970 statistic. Of this 1.1. million, 500,000 are African Americans. Some experts contend that imprisonment rates have now started to level off, but it is still projected that 300,000 more prisoners will be added by 1995. It costs $20 billion annually to keep these 1.1 million people in prison. Each week 1,100 new inmates are added nationally. The prison population increased 6.5 percent in the period from 1990 to 1991.

The National Center on Institutions and Alternatives advocates and supplies supervised rigorous probation, restitution, counseling, job training, and boot camps—intermediate punishments for certain convicted criminals whose background suggests these methods would work. It believes the public wants prison for violent criminals and stricter alternatives than simply supervised probation. Other reform advocates concur.[2]

From 1980 to 1990, a total of $30 billion was spent on prison construction. Even so, the prison population is 140,000 over capacity. Prison costs $10,000 to $30,000 a year depending on the state, but it costs $3,000 for strict probation, $5,500 for probation plus community service, $4,500 for house arrest, and $8,500 for boot camp.

In addition, many people are being incarcerated basically for being insolent and having a bad attitude when they are arrested on just a minor misdemeanor. Headlines tell of monthly or annual increases or decreases in crime, but even when crime decreases, as it did somewhat in the mid-1980s,[3] it is still a source of fear in many communities.

UCLA's James Q. Wilson writes persuasively on crime.[4] For twenty years, he has struggled with the data and assumptions behind everyone's favorite theories. According to Wilson, demographics tell a lot in predicting and explaining trends and changes in crime. Males eighteen to thirty are found to commit most crimes; this is not surprising since the more youth proportionately in the population, the higher the crime rate. This proportion crested in 1982, but began to decline because of birth patterns in the late 1950s and early 1960s.

Therefore, crime is likely to "naturally" recede in the 1990s from the levels it reached in the late 1970s.[5] But it is still too high and remains a major social obstruction. Crime cost $5 billion annually in lost wages, property, and medical expenses. A murder occurs roughly every twenty-three minutes.[6] There are over 20,000 murders a year. One out of 12,000 Americans is murdered each year, and half the victims know their assailants. Seventy-five percent are men, 53 percent are white, and 42 percent black. People under seventeen are committing increasingly more serious crimes. Violence in the schools has no parallels elsewhere in the world; it is also unprecedented in history.

Incorrigibles are defined as those who will return to prison within three years; they account for 30 percent of the prison population. Texas, California, New York, and Florida have 33 percent of all state prisoners. Each has over 25,000 prisoners. Sentences are getting longer, they are often mandatory, and parole is not as easily granted as it was earlier. Women, too, are going to prison in record numbers. By the 1980s they made up 4 percent or 17,000, of all prisoners, a figure double that of the decade before. The increase for males during that period was 70 percent.

The daily press issues a constant flow of crime statistics—so much so that they hardly register anymore and it is taken for granted that the United States has a big crime problem. Statistics have to be treated cautiously, however. In part, the changes simply reflect shifts in how crimes are reported. Yet, even allowing for inaccuracies, biases, and politically motivated manipulation, we do have an unacceptable problem.

Apparently many crimes are never reported. In addition, violent crime tends to go unpunished. State laws, police, and prosecution are inadequate, and even when criminals are caught, prosecution is difficult. A federal study found that 28 percent of witnesses fear reprisal and refuse to cooperate. In a New York study, 26 percent of victims were threatened. The ABA Committee on Victims wants stronger laws and new programs to prevent fear from subverting justice. Those citizens, who can identify hoodlums should not be frightened into silence.

According to the National Council on Aging, older people are more concerned about crime than about income and health.[7] The National Retired Teachers Association and the American Association of Retired Persons give self-help crime prevention training to members.

The United States has the highest incarceration rates and longest sentences in the industrial world. To date, 500,000 people are in prison, with 1,100 added a week. Although prisons costing billions have been built, we might still not have enough space for all the persons committed.[8] In the last thirty years, the average sentence has risen from sixteen to forty-five months. The problem is that high-probability punishment (the high risk of getting sentenced and serving time) deters crime and long, severe sentences do not seem to do much. Moreover, a high percentage of convicted criminals get probation: for example, 80 percent in New York and 50 percent in Pittsburgh. Thus, we do have high rates of incarceration, but we also have high rates of probation.[9] We can therefore conclude that conventional law enforcement and prisons are not enough. Something creative is needed to augment them, but to create innovations that work we need to know what we are really dealing with.

WHAT MOTIVATES CRIMINALS?

Elroy McGlothen, the former principal of Jordan High School in Watts, claims that kids join gangs because "in many cases it's for the same reasons people join Kiwanis and Rotary." Stanton Samenow,[10] a prison psychiatrist, says that criminals think differently and have "mercurial" attitudes toward others. To them, the question is how do other people serve the criminal's needs?

Although no one factor can be said to "cause" crime, several factors strongly correlate with high crime rates: economic conditions, family break-ups, drug availability and addiction, lack of family discipline, specific individual educational and employment history, insufficient crime prevention and law enforcement, demographic patterns, lenient courts, overcrowded jails, too few police in a jurisdiction, and not enough explanatory and persuasive information to criminals reminding them to "Behave Yourself."[11] A favorite theory is that unemployment, crowded and marginal housing, especially public housing, and ineffective school systems produce crime. Solve all that, it is said, and you will drastically reduce crime, goes the argument. In the best of all possible worlds it might, but given our political and budgetary realities it cannot happen that way. According to the same theory, increased crime reflects a class war between the poor and middle classes. Disparities in income and life-style create resentment and add to the potential for crime. There may be something to this theory, but it only marginally explains the kind of crime experienced daily in the United States.

The most likely victims of muggings are low-income, low-educated women, usually African American, living alone, and in poor health. With their meager resources, they cannot possibly represent a potential source of a large ripoff. In their case, the motives are more complex than stealing purely for money.

Some economists report that up to 25 percent of the income of black men 15 to 24 comes from crime. They see crime as more or less an alternative to legitimate work. Accepting this kind of economic reasoning would require that crime simply be accepted as a rational alternative to legitimate employment. Another motivation theory is that crime is primarily about affiliation, self-image, expression, and acceptance. It is not committed primarily to generate income per se. Yet another theory holds that bank robberies, muggings, and burglaries are fads much like graffiti. They peak when crime becomes fashionable and is the "in thing." According to this thinking, it is a phenomenon in social psychology, much like disco dancing, goldfish swallowing, hula hoops, or skateboards.

Over $40 million is stolen from financial institutions in some years. Do economic conditions like high inflation and recession drive more people to rob banks? In some cases, perhaps, yes, but there is no consistent, high, direct correlation between economic conditions and bank robberies. Yet there is evidence that bank robbery is faddish.

When people retreat from downtown at night, they leave it to the criminals. Extreme defensiveness is counterproductive for removing the countervailing presence of law-abiding citizens simply increases the potential for crime. In this environment faddish crime thrives. Wolfpacks and roving gangs have become "stylish" in Philadelphia and other cities.[12] Ten to twenty hoodlums, for example, may attack and complete a quick beating and robbery. Afterward, identification is difficult even if suspects are taken into custody. Wolfpacking reduces the criminals' risks. Obviously, criminals do want cash, but there's also a social drive to participate in the latest craze. The need to follow fads and to belong are basic desires. And crime does seem to meet the need. Still the matter remains debatable.

Another theory is that peer pressure induces crime. Crime generates excitement, especially for bored young criminals, and so crime becomes a social rite of passage with increased status as the objective. According to this view, juvenile crime and vandalism is a performance, a kind of theater that improves self-esteem. People with low self-esteem have few work or school-related chances to show their value, and so they "do" crime.

Then, what about drugs?[13] Is crime higher among drug users? One might suppose so. "Drug wars" was the common explanation for the wave of shootings in some big cities in the late 1980s and early 1990s. Criminologists say drug users are more likely to jump bail and more likely to commit robberies. Yet they are no more likely to try burglary, auto theft, arson, and property destruction than nonusers.[14]

RACIAL FACTORS

Now how does race figure in?[15] Crime varies by race, perhaps because of differences in legitimate opportunities, in taste for risk, and in treatment in the criminal justice system. Perhaps any outsiders such as African Americans will try crime at disproportionately high levels. In some cities as many as 80 percent of those arrested for murder, rape, and robbery are African American or Hispanic. Samuel Myers, a black economist at the University of Minnesota, attributes statistical differences primarily to discrimination in the criminal justice system. Yet he finds that correcting discrimination, especially in employment, may have little or no effect because the causes are so complex. If that is correct, a favorite theory of many people becomes invalid. Many liberal activists still argue that job discrimination is a primary cause, and many summarize the cause of much crime as racism, pure and simple.

According to another theory, temptation and frustration are the keys. People desire property that they cannot acquire and so they commit crime. In this distorted romantic view, the flaunting of wealth thus leads to Robin Hoodism. To others, however, the inability or unwillingness to defer gratification, a lower class deficiency, is the problem. Income inequity may explain some crime, but it's a lame excuse for leniency. Or perhaps the opportunity to steal is just greater these days. Home burglaries have increased as women enter the work force. Most forced entries occur between 10:00 A.M. and noon, and 1:00 P.M. and 3:00 P.M. in unattended homes.

Others theorize that the young thief feels despair, alienation, unfairness, and hopelessness. In that case, moral exhortations would fall on the deaf ears of people who do not share mainstream values. They fear getting caught, but they don't fully believe their stealing is wrong under the circumstances. Feeling they have been wronged by society, they believe they are entitled to get even.

What about genetics? Are some people genetically doomed to criminality? Some investigators believe that chromosomal differences may differentiate violent criminals, so that violent criminals could be identified at birth. Once identified, they could be treated medically and socially.

Finally, how does family influence criminality? An unwanted, unloved child is often a frustrated person in an impoverished home. From sun to sun, such a person's life is dominated by unemployment, illiteracy, alcoholism, drugs, abuse, family violence, and general pandemonium. In such a setting, who can think about self-improvement? As children, people learn that violence is the way to settle things, and so it is that, twenty years later, a full-fledged thug emerges. Some studies find that, regardless of intelligence, people from such backgrounds who go to jail become hardened.[16] It is difficult to reform them. Experts who work with them say they tend to be pessimistic. Their attitudes, sense of humor, offhand comments, and casual conversation all indicate they do not want to change.

So, there we have eleven general factors—poverty, faddish peer pressure, drugs, rational individual self-interest, racism, sheer opportunism, temptation, frustration, broad psychological factors like alienation, genetics, and family problems. Some of these motivational theories help us think about practical prevention; others lead only to rationalization and apology. Yet other factors contribute, that are only dimly perceived.

WHY DO CRIMINALS STOP?

Studies find that juvenile delinquents who reform seldom attribute their conversion to fear of police. They just review their behavior as they get older, change how they see themselves, and decide—"that's it. It was fun, but it isn't appropriate for an adult." Two key ideas here can help prevent crime. They commit crimes essentially for fun, and they rethink their behavior as they get older. Perhaps then we should take the fun out of it, and they should be given more time to think about it earlier. Much crime occurs because it is not made clear in both *word* and *action* that society disapproves. In effect, political and social leaders need to tell criminals "don't do that." Behave Yourself. Getting that message across will take us a long way.

We can prevent crime, and thereby help pay the debt and restore the economy, by investing in four quality tools: standard law enforcement, innovative law enforcement and prison programs, social service reforms, and innovative persuasive information. We have scrimped on all of these; to solve the problem, money is needed. Here is a courageous or foolish forecast, depending on your perspective. In ten or twenty years, crime in Washington, Harlem, Newark, Detroit, Los Angeles, Philadelphia, Houston, Boston, Miami, and Atlanta will be at levels so remarkably low that it will be hard to believe that back in 1993 people were afraid to walk alone through Central Park or to use the New York subways after dark.

IMPROVE CONVENTIONAL LAW ENFORCEMENT

Once upon a time there was a police chief in Philadelphia named Frank Rizzo. He was tough. One day he decided to run for mayor, and he was elected. During the campaign he often talked about crime. He promised that if elected, "I'll make Attila the Hun look like a faggot!" The radio call-in talk shows were busy for days after that one. Rizzo the Rampager crushing crime. And there have been others. David Duke in Louisiana, Ed Meese, Spiro Agnew, John Mitchell, George Bush. All tried to capitalize on the public's legitimate concerns about crime, but are busting heads, sensational raids, and a police policy of funky force really the optimum approach? The swaggering style may turn voters on, but does it prevent crime?

We have considered the prevailing ideas about what causes crime—both the more rarified and the common sense ideas. Here are basic steps that could help reduce crime, at least if they were given time, money, and support. Of course, thinking we have a remedy can be self-delusion; therefore, we should be confident and experimental in using these tools.

We want to reduce crime so that we can rehabilitate housing, run effective schools, create flourishing businesses, and create jobs. Local officials need to experiment, innovate, borrow ideas that work elsewhere, and create a tailored package of programs to fit the local situation. It is surprising how insular public officials can be, but even some conventional practices remain controversial. That is because crime prevention is still more art than science. Local practice can be improved by noticing what is being tried and working elsewhere. As Yogi Berra said, "You can learn a lot just by watching." However, it is more important that in convicting and sentencing criminals we not make the mistake of convicting one innocent person? Or is it more important to clear the streets of criminals even if we make a mistake now and then and jail an innocent person? Depending on where we come out on that question, we'll opt for either tougher or more lenient incarceration. We have to know where we stand on this age-old question before we can think through our positions on crime prevention and act.

STOP VIOLENCE AND SERIOUS CRIME

Police must be carefully selected and then trained fully. Then they have to be freed to deal with serious crime. Minor crimes can be handled in other ways. Twenty percent of arrests are for public drunkenness, a condition that should instead be dealt with by hospitals and clinics. That would free 20 percent more police time for patrol, investigation, and arresting criminals. People who commit violent crimes must be sent to jail. Such crime in New York State might drop 66 percent if everyone convicted spent three years in jail.

Some prominent law enforcement experts say we need to reform the system along these lines:

- Restore the concept of "future danger" based on the particular crime and past record.
- Have quicker trials.
- Limit appeals, with subsequent reviews only for claims of miscarriage of justice.
- Strengthen rehabilitation.

- Put first-time nonviolent offenders on supervised probation.
- Improve prisons.
- Allow family visitation.
- Counsel after release to develop self-respect, respect for others, accountability, and appreciation of work, thrift, and family.

Civil liberties lawyers believe that several of those proposals present threats to constitutional guarantees. However, the proposals try to balance care for criminal rights, community security, and sensitive incarceration for the dangerous. Moving in this direction will not produce Nirvana, but it will zero in on the major troublemakers.

In recent years, the federal government has spent 50 percent of its $450 million on juvenile delinquency prevention counsel and support, on truants, curfew violators, and incorrigibles. Most of these people are not especially violent. They are not the people who first come to our minds when we think of criminals in the streets. Although only 4 percent are violent, they are the ones we want caught, punished, and, if possible rehabilitated. Hence, our major prevention programs miss the mark. We seem to be working to rehabilitate those who are lower risk to begin with. The violent, on the other hand, go to jail, get out in short order, and then often strike again. "Career criminal" programs are common sense and effective. A handful of repeaters, with dozens of arrests and convictions, are the problem. Spotting them when they show up in court and making sure they are sentenced securely and don't slip through the cracks is a good basic attack on crime. Those who do well in training programs, demonstrating knowledge and talent, should be guaranteed a job when they get out. We need more and better jails, as well as rehabilitation, job counseling, and training as a package.

IT TAKES MORE MONEY

Voters resist paying for programs. They want crime solved and do not see the connection between crime and the economy's overall performance. Restitution theory should clarify that relationship. The problem is further compounded when corporate executives who have influence and political figures who are supposed to lead fail to lend their clout to proven or innovative programs. That has to change. The social debt justifies the extra expenditures for quality. The payoff will be a far stronger work force, enhanced corporate performance, and reduced bills for policing and security over the long run.

CONTROL HANDGUNS

The gun control issue is highly emotional. Many argue that if guns are outlawed, only the outlaws will have guns. Yet, we do not all need weapons to preserve law and order. Today 52 percent of all Americans own guns. Handgun-related crime can be cut by strict gun control. Some believe that other factors in law enforcement and long-term social trends are the chief reason behind the high crime statistics. Many don't like gun control on principle, but controlling handguns, making them tough to buy and requiring their registration, makes sense.

With a little imagination and a solid rationale, we can regain a harmonious social atmosphere. If we understand crime's role in economic development, we can reduce it dramatically.

8

Discourage Immature Parenting and Welfare Dependency

If you can't feed your baby, then don't have a baby. And don't think maybe, if you can't feed your baby.
—Michael Jackson, "Wanna Be Startin' Somethin'"

God bless the child that's got his own.
—Billie Holliday

The federal budget, as well as most state and municipal budgets, are too heavily burdened by direct and indirect costs that could be avoided. These costs support people whose indiscretions, irresponsibility, and self-indulgence have put them in difficult circumstances. By drastically curtailing this willful conduct, much of the groaning economic load on the public sector could be lifted. These people will be freed to develop into productive participants living satisfying, rewarding lives.

The economy is dragged down by the social and real economic costs caused by thoughtless procreation. The social debt can be paid in part by investing in programs that will stop this waste and misery.

BEHAVE YOURSELVES

The strategy should include powerful persuasive communications that make it clear that getting pregnant unprepared is not acceptable; that everyone is expected to stay in school, study, and participate fully in the adult employment world; that with few exceptions, no one should start a family alone; and that no couple should start a family until they have each completed high school, each worked for three years, and each saved at least $5,000. These Behave Yourself standards, or other standards with the same intent, can be broadcast and reinforced in such a way that they become the universal rule. They can overcome social forces that discourage sensible, mature planning, self-control, and discipline.

By the early 1990s more and more big city school systems had seen the consequences of a hands-off approach to values training.[1] As a result, they decided to step into the vacuum to promote strong values with concentrated programs and to reinforce responsibility, self-control, and maturity over the low-life values of the environment.[2]

Elijah Anderson teaches sociology at the University of Pennsylvania, and in 1990 he published a research paper in the *Annals of the American Academy*.[3] He found that young black males in particular play games with sex. They use deceit, are out to "get over," and generally behave unethically. Their lack of values has to be discredited as part of any campaign of renewal, and honorable dealings have to be strengthened. Another voice urging social restraint is Virginia's Douglas Wilder, the nation's first black governor. In 1991 he was also one of the first prominent black leaders to urge and promote substance and sexual abstinence among young people.[4] That message is vital and needs to be amplified.

Yet another impetus for leading black youth away from social danger is Values and Choices, a program designed to help middle school (seventh and eighth grade) students resist peer pressure and decide on sex, drug, alcohol, and other value-based matters with confidence. Some of its techniques are so-called "scare tactics." Some of its other approaches have won the praise of members of the National Association of Abstinence Education.

Policies must be instituted to reverse deterioration and self-defeating behavior. To succeed in this effort, two things must be understood. First, declining competitiveness and productivity are in part a function of the have nots' social problems. Second, those social problems and associated economic damage are, in turn, partly a function of the social debt. We have not understood the relationships and until we get those connections clear, we will continue to flounder. Although the reports and TV specials mentioned accurately described situations, they did not diagnose and prescribe effectively.

The National Urban League runs a Male Responsibility Program that uses posters and broadcasts that communicate self-control. "Don't Make a Baby If You Can't Be a Father. Be Careful. Be Responsible." Planned Parenthood has a similar campaign. This kind of message can help turn it around. League President John Jacobs recommends the direct approach —blunt talk using sophisticated media. He believes this method should work where other approaches have not, and he is probably right.

The schools, too, should do their part. Harvard's School of Public Health has a Center for Health Communication that uses TV and other media to teach the public how to keep well and teach health experts how to better explain complex health issues. There is a real place for clear, simple explanation. Schools should also teach values. Coordinated sophisticated programs in schools, reinforcing integrity, truth, personal accountability, and respect for others' rights, are also part of the Behave Yourself strategy.

No one under twenty-one should have a child, and no one who has not finished high school, worked three years successfully, found a committed partner, and saved a nest egg should have a child. Those are not particularly stringent requirements; they are simply common sense. If they are made the basis for a sustained campaign, they can catch on and be accepted. Instead, some people tolerate and encourage irresponsibility. Early unplanned pregnancy, family disintegration, and chronic welfare dependency are the result. They defeat attempts to stimulate the economy, improve productivity, and compete. We know at a gut level what's needed, but the national leaders have not asked voters to provide dollars to produce the information and counseling campaign that is needed. The money to do that is owed; paying it is in everyone's interest.

THE POWER OF WORDS

Communications, which could be a splendid supplement to personal, family, church, neighborhood, and community sanctions, has been a tremendous underused tool in improving behavior. One reason why we have social problems, of course, is that old-fashioned person-to-person local sanctions have been undermined. We therefore need to reinforce them, and we can do that with sophisticated mass media. Community, political, business, and religious leaders can also help by repudiating negative attitudes and behavior.

When young people from rural backgrounds suddenly enter the urban culture, few have the requisite knowledge and orientation to cope with their novel situation. They seldom understand the new standards they have to meet. Education and reinforcement can help them make the transition quicker and more successfully.

There are limits to what government can or should do about social control. Some people, for example, advocate that a license be issued to parenthood: a government license would have to be obtained before anyone had a baby. While that is quite an excessive notion, the right kind of public investments in constructive behavior could help pay some of the social debt.

The National Urban League, the NAACP, and organizations like Kappa Alpha Psi, Alpha Phi Alpha, Delta Sigma Theta, Omega Psi Phi and other sororities and fraternities, the Children's Defense Fund, the National Council of Negro Women—all want to put an end to family breakdown. By forming partnerships with government and corporations, together they can discourage irresponsible early childbirth and ignorance in parenting.

An important ingredient in any comprehensive program is the ability to reach not only girls but also boys. Such a program is the Mott Foundation which supports the Teen Outreach Program to prevent teen pregnancy in St. Louis high schools. In general, the have nots are not as easily influenced by others' opinions as are middle-class people, but many can be reached with solid, well-designed information campaigns. They get fifty-seven varieties of messages every day; advertisers come at them in waves. Thus, information campaigns have to get through the noise, grab attention, and provoke word-of-mouth reactions.

To promote Behave Yourself, it is essential to explain why it is better to conform. Too many political and social leaders still dwell on the "reasons" why people mess up. They explain endlessly, basing their rationalizations on their feeling that the poor are victims. But that approach reinforces helplessness.

Race awareness, class consciousness, and feelings like alienation help determine attitudes about how to behave. Moreover, many poor people resist social authority. Here the old folk song comes to mind: "Mama don't allow no banjo playing here. But I don't care what Mama don't allow, I'm gonna play my banjo anyhow." Too many people want to play their banjos despite the rules, but if we know what we value and why, we can offer good guidelines for successful living. Perhaps banjo playing is not so terrible, but we don't need to be reticent about declaring rules for living that make sense and should be followed by everyone.

In the 1980s, the National Urban League set out to reduce teen pregnancy and help female-headed households. The League wanted middle-class and professional people to volunteer to counsel youngsters and poor people, one on one, face to face. They have their work cut out for them. Some experts think many young mothers have children because they want a government check each month, they face peer pressure, they have a psychological need for love and respect that is not coming from parents, siblings, or male friends and lovers, and they are ignorant of effective birth control. Pregnant teenagers cost $8 billion in welfare. There are also 1 million abortions annually, half by teenagers. Another sad statistic is that teen childbearing rose in the 1980s, and many decided to keep the babies.

What else can be done? Schools, churches, and Planned Parenthood can educate teens about birth control and abortion, or abstention. Family planning, sex education, promotion of contraceptives—all work. But does ignorance really lead to teen pregnancy? Experts report that 50 percent of pregnancies happen during the first six months of sexual activity. That is when young women are still ambivalent about having sex. They deny that they are sexual. It takes awhile for them to be comfortable with this behavior. It is during this time that they frequently get pregnant. However, the problem is not simply that they have no knowledge of how to prevent pregnancy. Therefore, straight, technical information alone is not all that is missing. Many parents are uncomfortable talking about sex with teens. This contributes to the guilt and delays contraceptive use. Consequently, public education programs should also aim at parents, encouraging them to advise their teenagers that contraception is important.

Charles Murray[5] argues that welfare liberalization helped loosen social controls. He's probably right, but by putting out the right information, in the right way, we can restore the idea that people who are not prepared to be fully responsible should not bear children.

"BEHAVE YOURSELF" WILL IMPROVE THE ECONOMY

Cities try to attract industry, hold companies making noises about leaving, revitalize declining industrial, commercial, and neighborhood shopping districts, and create a climate that encourages small business investment and growth. They also hold conferences and workshops to outline their financial incentives and to spotlight amenities. Tax incentives, enterprise zones, grants, and industrial revenue bonds all have value, for they can alter location decisions. On the other hand, we pay too little attention to how residents' behavior affects location decisions. This factor gets subsumed under "quality of life" or "available labor skills." The problem, however, is not simply one of skill and training—it's character. To business decision makers, that can overshadow tax gimmicks. Are too many potential employees actually unemployable because of their attitude, including hostile, impatient, unruly, discourteous, and unethical behavior. In other words, are they "a pain in the ass" to have around? People with low technical skills can be trained; writing and computational skills can be developed, as can mechanical and clerical abilities. The skills that really concern potential employers when they talk euphemistically about the "labor force," however, are skills in social interaction and self-control.

Economic development officers should explicitly put the work ethic and ethics in personal relations on the agenda. Local economic development groups and chambers of commerce should pay attention to the role of behavior in restoring industry and retailing vitality. Behavior should join tax abatement, zoning variance, land writedown, and lease back in economic development planning.

Most people can be friendly, and even when they are not, most can be agreeable. For sometimes complex reasons, however, many people are difficult, unpleasant, and grouchy, and most avoid interacting with them. Thus decisions on site location are influenced not only by crime, but also by the hassle factor. While financial incentives and good administration help industrial development authorities stimulate growth, it is important to emphasize the improved behavior of clerks, and semiskilled, and unskilled workers also attracts investors. That, too, helps revitalize local economies.

Some experts contend that it is pointless to invest big sums to revitalize older inner cities. Instead, natural processes should be allowed to work, so that ultimately property is abandoned and residents are dislocated. Economic forces will produce new supply and demand conditions. New tastes will produce new activities, and we will not need public subsidies. Others counter that massive investments should be made to save these areas. Still others advocate a blend of these two strategies: some investment and some abandonment.

To get favorable outcomes, we must concentrate on the missing ingredient: rehabilitate the people in chronically distressed areas. Helping young people lead disciplined lives benefits everyone. Reducing crime and increasing self-control, including matters like delaying childbearing and being effective parents, will pay off. That is because budget items for welfare, police, sanitation, public housing, firefighting, and more are actually determined by how well people behave. As behavior improves, it will cost less to run cities. If we invest to improve behavior, we will discover that those are the best alternatives for stimulating economic and business development, creating jobs, and, ultimately, lowering local taxes.

9

Invest in Persuasive Communications

The best thing you can do for the poor is not to be one of them
—Reverend Ike

Effective communication can sell just about everything
—Barbara Bush

We have seen how behavior undermines economic development in distressed areas, and we have also reviewed how self-defeating behavior ruins economic performance generally and helps drag down overall performance. Our proposed remedy should be comprehensive. We need to pay restitution, and the payments should be in capital investments— in housing, health, business development, training and education. They should also be in innovative law enforcement and programs that directly seek to reverse behavior dysfunction.

Let us use Madison Avenue techniques to persuade everyone to behave themselves. They should be asked to obey the law, delay and plan families, get education, work and save, and protect their health. Public and private funds should be used to pay for the best communications talent, talent that should design and implement programs to use all media to convey values convincingly. This is a form of education and is one way to help pay the debt. It is also an investment that will strengthen the economy, both directly and indirectly.

The Ad Council has proven the value of persuasive communications on some problems. Since the late 1980s, it has led a campaign against drinking and driving, sponsored by the National Highway Traffic Safety Administration.[1] Thomas A. Hedrick, president of the Media-Advertising Partnership for a Drug Free America, notes that the media are more interested in running public service spots than they used to be "because the quality of the messages is improving dramatically."[2] There it is. That's the key.

In 1990 radio donated $500 million and broadcast TV $463 million of time for such campaigns. Free bus stop and other outdoor advertising provided $100 million, and cable TV another $135 million. The time and space are therefore available. The National Crime Prevention Council ran free TV ads in 1991 on the hit TV show, "Designing Women." In addition, the networks have freed up more such prime time for good causes on shows like "Who's the Boss?" and even on the World Series.[3] Of course, this happened during an economic slump when airtime went begging. The Ad Council reported that in 1991 a total of $1.3 billion of such time and print space was donated. By 1992 the Partnership for a Drug Free America ran ads at the rate of $1 million a day. The Teenage Mutant Ninja Turtle ads against drugs have effectively aired this way. Magazines and newspapers have also given such space. Thus, the chance to do social marketing economically is especially good in bad times, although the possibility exists throughout the business cycle.

Although people can be persuaded to identify their interests with group interests, socially cooperative behavior has been dropping for thirty years.[4] Income tax compliance, TV news watching, newspaper readership, charitable contributing, voting—all middle-class indicators—have also been down. The problem extends beyond the have nots. Common courtesy is also in decline. Actually, England has a Polite Society that tries to promote civility. It cites an insurance company study finding that 47 percent of all road accidents in England can be traced to an earlier act of driver discourtesy.[5] Thus, human attitudes do have serious behavioral and economic consequences.

In the 1980s the Ohio Governor's Office of Criminal Justice used social marketing in an attempt to combat serious crime. All media, print and electronic, were used to persuade criminals to end their activities. The campaign, developed by Lang, Fisher and Stashower Advertising, emphasized consequences, an approach that should be refined, strengthened, and used nationally. During the ads' first six months crimes in which guns are used declined in Cleveland by 36 percent. Florida, California, and New York have also adopted this approach, with unknown results.

ADS AGAINST DRUGS

The American Association of Advertising Agencies, the 4As, is working to reduce drug use through a public interest campaign which it has called the "biggest single undertaking of the advertising community since World War II." 4As is involved in a Media-Advertising Partnership for a Drug Free America along with the Advertising Council, the Association of

National Advertisers, and the American Advertising Federation. Prime-time TV slots are donated by the networks, and print media like *Newsweek* are also involved.

Advertising is not all powerful, even though it involves astronomical outlay. On average, $85 to $100 billion a year is spent on ads, and individuals receive 200,000 messages a year, 600 a day. Of those, we may notice 75, and remember 12, 3 negatively and 9 positively. Despite these limitations, it is a tool that will improve behavior and upgrade the work force. For example, in 1982 Baltimore's police commissioner went on a late-night radio call-in talk show to talk about narcotics. On the show he invited listeners to phone in tips on pushers and dealers. He expected a light response, but was deluged. That night his police rounded up many unsuspecting criminals. He should not have been surprised by the effectiveness of the exercise. That is the untapped power of information: it can help us solve many a tough social problem. In the 1980s television was used to bring out our better angels, but there's more to do. Informing viewers of higher standards is a noble use for TV.

SOCIAL MARKETING

The researchers who have laid the analytical groundwork for this concept of media social marketing include Ronald Berman,[6] Seymour Fine,[7] and Philip Kotler.[8] They all explain how information can be important in reducing destructive behavior. A Department of Justice report gives further reason to use information campaigns. "Media Campaigns and Crime Prevention" is about campaigns like McGruff the Crime Dog's, "take a bite out of crime" public service announcements.

James Q. Wilson discusses family problems as causes of crime in his classic *Thinking About Crime* and asks what can be done about broken homes anyhow: "What agency do we create, what budget do we allocate that will supply the missing parental affection and restore to the child consistent discipline by a stable and loving family?"[9] Information is part of the answer. We can persuade and reinstate discipline, and we can also remind adults and young people of what society expects. In that sense, information will do some of what families fail to do.

The Justice Department periodically conducts campaigns on how poten-tial victims can avoid being victims. Campaigns are also needed to get criminals to stop their activities. Enough experiments along these lines have worked to give us some reason for optimism. We can "advertise" to obey the law, and many criminals will comply. It depends on a key assumption—that most know right from wrong and that they know what Behave Yourself means. Because many criminals and potential criminals are never reminded, sophisticated information can remind them effectively.

CAN CELEBRITIES PROMOTE "BEHAVE YOURSELF?"

What if famous black personalities like Bill Cosby, Dr. J., O. J. Simpson, Michael Jackson, Bo Jackson, Michael Jordan, Oprah Winfrey, Spike Lee, Diana Ross, Cecily Tyson, Public Enemy, Hammer, and Stevie Wonder, as well as white and Hispanic youth culture heroes like New Kids on the Block, U2, and Madonna, Bruce Springsteen, Bart Simpson, Hulk Hogan, Joe Montana, Santana, Clint Eastwood, John Travolta, Gloria Estefan, and Sylvester Stallone, did first-rate, award-winning quality commercials against heavy crime? Picture Arsenio Hall in a polished prime-time commercial whose message is: obey the law and don't commit burglary. Or Burt Reynolds or Chita Rivera in a thirty-second spot on armed robbery. If these are not the right people, then many others can be picked. But Madison Avenue techniques can persuade and inform. This approach can work as we have seen when used against drugs, drinking, and shoplifting. Can it be as effective against felony crimes and other destructive behavior?

If in the past ten years, O. J. Simpson could sell Hertz rental cars, Ray Charles Diet Pepsi, Bill Russell long-distance telephone use, Joe Namath pantyhose and Hamilton Beach small appliances, can well-known figures also sell Behave Yourself—compliance with the law and honorable, cooperative, constructive behavior? Can entertainment and sports figures help? The experts conclude that the answer depends on how mass-communicated admonitions or suggestions match up with the way viewers see their own world, and how much they identify with these celebrities. Although we have used the media to help change certain behaviors, we have not used them to deal with violent crimes and heavy felonies. Social marketing to encourage witness cooperation has been tried. Some spots used a black actor, James McEachern, but they lacked high production values. The low-budget look diminished effectiveness, because they lacked the visual qualities that have since been recognized as key.

Of course, celebrities are not our salvation, but they are definitely part of the answer. Some disagree. *Advertising Age* states that celebrity endorsement of products has little lasting impact. David Ogilvy, a leading advertiser, also believes that celebrities have little selling power. Therefore, whether they will have much effect on crime through an idea campaign cannot be guaranteed. Experts differ. All the same, they're one arrow in our quiver.

MARKETING IMAGINATION

Theodore Levitt,[10] marketing professor at Harvard Business School, has presented a concept, creative marketing strategy, that will be useful in any attempt to explain, inform, and persuade people to change life-styles and to adopt constructive behavior. Levitt's marketing imagination concept allows us to look at the world and its problems in a way that sparks creative responses. It is an attitude, a point of view, and we need it to reduce destructive behavior.

In selling goods and services or ideas, we try to establish a relationship; the sale is not the end of it. When we buy a car, we expect satisfying, ongoing service. So it is with social marketing. If criminals begin to change, in exchange they will expect institutions to respond to them credibly, consistently, and satisfactorily. Schools, jobs, and opportunities will have to become responsive, or "customer loyalty" will not be built and sustained. Society will incur an obligation to come through constructively. That does not mean a blatant quid pro quo—"a job or I'll keep on mugging." However, a new chance at satisfaction will be implied if we ask for improved behavior.

In 1982 a widely viewed one-hour TV special, the "National Crime and Violence Test," told about crime prevention and how to survive if attacked.[11] The show included questions and answers with comments by experts and by convicted felons. That approach has larger possibilities.

American business spends $70 billion on advertising a year, but still we are not sure whether advertising works. While an ad's memorableness can be measured, it is only an indirect way to judge whether it influences behavior. Advertising can remind us of desires, wants, needs, values, and beliefs, which gives it power to improve behavior.

The Pennsylvania Committee for Effective Justice tries to deter crime by advertising on television, billboards, and transit to inform criminals of the state's mandatory sentencing laws. Philadelphia's district attorney thought that warning criminals that, if convicted, they would go to jail would serve as a deterrent. The average criminal, he asserts, thinks that the law is a joke, and so they need to learn differently. The message of the ad was: "Nobody is going to help you if you're convicted." The experiment cost $115,000, and the results are still inconclusive. Business groups put up the money for the ad, and the Pennsylvania Chamber of Commerce also helped. The legislature had voted against paying for it, but seeing the connection between crime prevention and productivity, competitiveness, economic development, and the well-being of all Americans might bring politicians to support such strategies.

Pennsylvania mandates a five-year jail term for using a gun in a felony, a five-year sentence for violent crimes after a record of violent crimes, mandatory life for second and third degree murder, and a five-year term for violent crimes on public transportation. Similar ad campaigns for such mandatory sentencing have cut crimes in Florida and Massachusetts.

Barry and Enright Productions, which produces game shows on television, also films dramatizations of actual crimes for use in news programs with help of the U.S. Marshalls. The ninety-second spots include a wanted poster of the fugitive and a toll-free phone number.[12]

Recently, New York City used social marketing in another campaign. "Take it from the champs, graffiti is for chumps," said a poster of local boxers Hector Camacho and Alex Ramos. "Fame is seeing your name in lights, not seeing it sprayed on the subway," said another poster of Irene Cara and Gene Ray, stars of the movie *Fame*. Dave Winfield, then of the Yankees, and Joe Frazier were also in the campaign. Chase Manhattan led the group paying for the campaign, and the National Paint and Coatings Association contributed cash.[13] Some observers who have looked into the motivations behind graffiti maintain that they don't believe these kinds of campaigns are based on a solid understanding of graffiti writers. They don't think graffiti writers will be much influenced when celebrities disapprove. Since graffiti is a form of personal display and protest and is basically antiestablishment, having heroes put it down will not work, they think.

SPREAD THE WORD

The point of good advertising is to influence people through word of mouth. Primary impact is important, of course, but the most important objective is to spread the word—not about how clever or unusual the spot is, but what the message is. Eighty percent of consumer decisions are based on someone's personal recommendation. Thomas Bonoma of Harvard Business School and Gordon Weaver of Paramount Pictures agree that word of mouth is the most important marketing element.

Calvin Klein jeans has run many controversial ads in the past decade, some of which say nothing at all. Instead, the actors in the spots talk about horses, babies, food—anything but jeans. After thirty seconds, a voice says, "Calvin Klein jeans." End of spot. Although Harold Levine, of Levine, Huntley, Schmidt, and Beaver, thought the ads were great, other professionals disagreed. Nonetheless, the campaign provoked word of mouth and news stories about the ad—publicity—and it promoted an image. Some viewers identified with the actors.

That is the objective with criminals, but this kind of unorthodox campaign takes talent, imagination, and the guts to withstand criticism. Would Richard Avedon and Doon Arbus, the creators, make use of social marketing against felony crime? Do their ads sell jeans? Sales increased after the campaign, but were the ads responsible? The general economy and seasonal factors also played a role. Would such ads work on crime? There's a good chance they might. We simply need to find out.

SOME CREATIVE ADVERTISING WORKS TO REDUCE MINOR CRIME

Virginia's Department of Litter Control uses radio, television, and print in its campaigns to reduce the problems of littering. In one ad, a family approaches a nail-studded piece of wood on the road. The mother screams. The car swerves out of control. Brakes screech. The frame freezes. Then comes the anti-litter message. Such striking dramatizations get important social information across to the public.[14] Richard Staelin of Duke University observes that clever ads can get a viewer to buy once, but they are less effective in encouraging repeat buying. So it is with social advertising: clever ads have their place, but solid information has to be presented. Gimmicks and grabbers alone won't do it. Recent research tells us that candor in advertising is potent. Crime prevention ads should tell it like it is about the costs and benefits of going straight.

In the 1980s Richard King Mellon Foundation and the Metropolitan Life Foundation funded a TV campaign in Pennsylvania to fight drug and alcohol abuse; the state secretary of education coordinated town meetings in conjunction with the TV spots; and Pittsburgh public television set up 100 community groups for followup. This kind of multilevel information with corporate participation, and state and local partners, is very important. Most creative people will work on social marketing anticrime campaigns free of charge.

In 1984, during the Super Bowl game, Apple Computer ran a bizarre and now famous ad. It was a scene from a movie, Orwell's *1984*. What did Big Brother have to do with the new MacIntosh personal computer? The ad touched an emotional button. So, too, can crime prevention advertising.

Michael Tesch of Ally and Gergano, an innovative firm, created a memorable Federal Express campaign. It featured a fast-talking, zonked-out executive. "Artful persuasion" is the concept. We don't "play with people's brains or talk down to them" says Emil Gergano. That's a good guiding philosophy for anticrime campaigns.

Following research on how people react to ads, Shepard Kurnit of Calet, Hirsch, Kurnit and Spector Inc., and his son, Paul, of Griffin Bacal Inc., concluded that people recognize quality in creativity and persuasiveness, much as do advertising professionals. Although no absolute formula exists for good ads, humor works and celebrities do too if the messages presented fit their personalities. A Stan Freberg anticrime campaign would be funny. Imagine the artful, effective spots he would conceive.

Until the 1920s, advertising did not attack directly; the idea was simply to be constructive and positive. That philosophy is now dead. Advertisers frequently put down competitors. Minute Maid, for example, says that Country Time is the "no lemon-lemonade," and Nature's Remedy claims that Ex-Lax contains an "artificial chemical." To grab the audience's attention, the idea is to knock competitors—hit hard, go for broke. Will that approach work in social marketing? Ads that badmouth crime and criminals might do the trick where polite information and explanation might not.

Program-length commercials are now familiar; Pac Man, Rubik's Cube, and G.I. Joe dolls, for instance, have produced half-hour cartoon shows. Often only a thin line separates programming and advertising. As a result, Action for Children's Television (ACT), the watchdogs of children's shows, has complained to the Federal Trade Commission. Program-length "ads" against crime and drugs might work. Specifically, they might encourage teenagers and young adults to stay in school, study, graduate, go to work, save money, get good experience, and wait until they're grownups before starting families.

COMIC HEROES

During World War II, comic books were used to market patriotic ideals and to promote self-sacrificing, collective effort. In 1954, however, congressional hearings zapped comic books for contributing to juvenile delinquency, and since then the industry has been sensitive. Now it again could help market noble ideas. Of course, Spiderman has been used by Planned Parenthood, and Superman by the American Lung Association. But there are unexplored areas, including violent crime, where comic heroes might inform and persuade. In the past the National Highway Safety Administration's campaigns to encourage seat belt use and to fight driving after drinking made use of Superman. That approach should be tried with felonies.

Since crime statistics are manipulated both administratively and politically it is hard to tell what works. All the same, ad campaigns have made criminals aware of the risks of a sure sentence, and that is enough reason to think we have a potent information tool that we're not using enough. The National Conference of Metropolitan Courts states that the public doesn't understand our legal system's basic principles, but we get ideas about courts and the law from the media. That is a tool that can enlighten and encourage rather than confuse and mislead.

QUID PRO QUO?

Marketing, in the broad sense, involves an exchange, usually goods or services for money, and marketing to improve behavior also requires opportunities for "exchange." Information on the benefits of improved behavior represents a kind of marketing exchange through which standards of behavior can be communicated. It also permits information about the consequences of violating the standards to be emphasized.

Information should be based on solid knowledge. What do poor, marginal, alienated, and fearful people want? What are their aspirations, tastes, and preferences? Information has to respond to audience desires, and, at the same time, it has to show that improved behavior will produce benefits. Thus, information on counseling, social services, vocational training, and real opportunities should be included. This will address real needs. The message, of course, will run into countermessages that encourage lawbreaking and irresponsibility. The marketplace of ideas is competitive. We won't have a monopoly on access to audiences.

MIXING MEDIA

Mass media information should be combined with pamphlets, billboards, transit ads, brochures, and face-to-face contacts. For example, Theater Without Bars in Trenton, New Jersey, is an ex-con group that performs in schools, churches, and civic groups. Another example is the Washington Redskins which has worked with local law enforcement agencies. They pass out football picture cards with crime prevention tips on the reverse. In some years police have passed out 3 million cards. The Dallas Cowboys, Miami Dolphins, and Los Angeles Rams have sponsored similar programs.

Publicity—unpaid advertising with no sponsor identified—can also be used, as can promotions, special events, and contests. However, campaigns can backfire if audiences have nothing to do with the interest generated. Audiences need outlets for their energies. They should be asked to do something that will improve their lot—not simply be preached at.

People who change behavior pay a price—either money, opportunity or energy or psychic costs. Criminals who give up theft, shoplifting, dope peddling, burglary or mugging pay a price in a sense: Criminals who go straight suffer both economic and psychic costs. Thus, information should persuade them that their cost-to-benefit ratio will improve. Obeying the law has to be attractive if only in psychic terms—that is the message to convey. No doubt, some people will resent such messages and feel manipulated. Because some experiments have backfired, great skill is needed. It would be inappropriate and unwise for businesses, churches, unions, civic groups, and political groups merely to use television to scold. We do not need media pointing down from heaven, nagging wrongdoers.

PUBLICIZE PUNISHMENTS

Publicizing appropriate punishments for crimes can serve as a powerful deterrent. Both the sentencing and incarceration of serious criminals should be front-page news and lead off the six o'clock news. Indeed, even executions might well be broadcast and televised. This might seem barbaric, but perhaps a few televised executions, handled right, could be a major deterrent to violent crime. Obviously, capital punishment is the subject of extensive emotional debate, but if executions for grossly heinous crimes were held, then it might be valuable to make sure would-be killers are visibly impressed, with accompanying explanation and discussion of background, context, and rationale.

The key here is information. Reminders and explanation, more than laws and regulations, will help people overcome temptation, social pressure, and bad habits, and Behave Themselves.

OTHER USES OF THE MEDIA

A number of campaigns aimed at changing behavior have been launched:

- Michael Whittaker, advertising director for the Boy Scouts of America, has used ads to recruit members. "Boy do we need Scouting" ads actually speak to audience concerns about behavior—crime, drug abuse, and lax discipline.
- The Ford Foundation donated $2 million to the Public Education Fund for the purpose of organizing public/corporate partnerships to support the public schools and to upgrade public perceptions of the schools.
- Portland, Oregon, offers some unique advice on its billboards: "If you're looking for a prostitute, plan on getting arrested."
- San Francisco's municipal transit system tries to embarrass fare cheaters into paying through billboards and posters that show a delinquent passenger getting heat from fellow passengers.
- The National Transportation Safety Board works with the states to get citizens to report drunk drivers.

Campaigns such as these have yet to be tried on heavier problems such as violent and property crime, which might also be reduced with powerful messages.

PERSUASION

The mode by which information actually influences behavior is still unclear, but the media are more likely to reinforce predispositions than to change them. Information programs to influence behavior try to establish a chain reaction to influence subsequent interpersonal communications. That is where the leverage is—word of mouth. How can new information get into those personal channels where it can persuade? The more campaigns generate word of mouth, the more information will get through. Although most media information supports our best predispositions, we can do better. The media can reinforce a weak sense of right and wrong with a basic message—Behave Yourself.

Most people rely on personal sources for guidance on medical issues, fashions, entertainment, and shopping but turn to experts when they need information on public issues. This suggests that indirect or personal means on personal behavior should be used to inform and persuade. Even people with chronic destructive behavior will turn to friends when they need personal advice. Thus, persuasion can begin with mass media information. Then it will rely on indirect personal influences. Conversion is a continuing process that lasts for weeks after exposure to an idea.

Messages can be ignored or given comfortable interpretations when they are unwelcome. The process is not one way. It is not a matter of simply producing information that will then do something to passive receivers. People are more susceptible to persuasion at critical junctures of their lives, such as when they enter the labor force or get married, or start families. The points at which people move from one life-style to another are points at which information can have maximum impact.

When we watch television, we may ignore the advertising, but with enough repetition the advertising works. Despite ourselves, we recall the name of the product and something about it. Then the next time we're in a store, the brand comes to mind and we buy it. After experience with the product, we internalize our new preference. This same process applies to ideas. Youth in poor communities, for example, can "try" new behavior to see how they like it. Later, they can alter attitudes to fit the new experience.

Ninety-five percent of low-income households have television; 100 percent have radios; 50 to 75 percent get a daily newspaper; and the average low-income black family reads two African-American periodicals. Therefore, getting information to people is not the problem. The challenge is finding the right message mix, designing campaigns, and then managing them effectively. For example, John Johnson, publisher of *Ebony* and *Jet*, could have tremendous impact on turning destructive behavior around by presenting well-timed cover stories on Behave Yourself.

SHOW, NOT JUST TELL

To increase people's resistance to lawbreaking and to inform them of constructive ways to live, we need to raise their self-esteem. If they feel they have enough self-control, they will persuade themselves and use the information. Since people are more easily persuaded when they figure things out for themselves, we need not preach. Instead, information should involve the audience. They will sort out values and examine behavior as they watch or listen to the message. Information can involve audiences as active rather than passive receivers. People who feel they have persuaded themselves to adopt better behavior will be solidly persuaded, and they will be unlikely to backslide.

Audience motives, tastes and behavior and the potential acceptance of new messages must be clearly understood. Otherwise, they can boomerang and harden attitudes by being too inconsistent with values. Persuasion also requires periods of rest while messages sink in. Conversely, a steady flow of messages can also be counterproductive. Information campaigns will have to take account of all factors that contribute to crime and social destructiveness.

LISTENING, WATCHING, AND READING

Poor people watch lots of TV. Frequently, they are under stress, feel frustrated, fatalistic, isolated, and alienated, and seek fantasy and escape. Thus it is that they turn to television. TV content is a major topic of conversation among many poor people. Most people respond to persuasive messages in the media by arguing back at TV sets, newspapers, or radio commercials. In the end, however, they often accept the message and are persuaded.

Adolescents in particular resort to advertising to learn how to behave. Ads do not only dispense information about products; they do much more. Behavior can therefore be heavily influenced by popular music, newspapers, film, television, comic books, magazines, billboards, transit advertising, cartoons, comic strips, and more. Thus far, research has not proved that popular song lyrics really influence behavior, but they probably do. During the 1992 presidential campaign, the uproar over Sister Souljah and other rap artists thought to be espousing violence and hatred showed that most people agree that communication is powerful. Let us therefore use it constructively.

TELL IT LIKE IT IS

Destructive behavior stems in part from dull perceptions or low consciousness. Many people who litter, break traffic laws, shoplift, or chronically perform poorly are simply unaware and need to be informed to raise their awareness of what is expected of them. No one can promise happiness, but the prospect that improved behavior will lead to benefits can be offered. The message must not be a con job, or an oversell, or promise quick solutions to complex problems. A vision of progress, however, will appeal to those who have never been invited to grow and be challenged.

This process of raising consciousness is similar to the processes used by the human potential movement with middle-class people to offer the potential of more rewarding living and responsibility. The poor and marginal can be helped through mass media and other information methods, much as many middle-income people are helped through expensive interpersonal methods. People must be made to see benefits in Behave Yourself. In some ways, that is similar to "getting in touch with ourselves."

THE BOTTOM LINE

Municipal budgets would be vastly more manageable if the behavior of all citizens were at middle-class levels. Behavior as it affects property maintenance, health, parenting, trash and garbage disposal, compliance with law, school attendance and performance, and traffic conduct must be improved. If the have nots can be persuaded to Behave Themselves in these areas, budgets could be greatly reduced, and most people would be more satisfied with day-to-day living. The economy would reflect the improved attitudes, and production would increase, giving everyone a brighter social outlook.

An important case in point is New York City's financial situation which has been rocky for two decades. There has been widespread concern about whether the city can successfully survive its austere periods without social repercussions. Many steps have been taken: a Municipal Assistance Corporation has been set up, and steps such as financial controls, higher transit fares, introduction of tuition at a previously free city university system, and new budget and financial directors from the private sector, have been put into place. New York City has endured layoffs of municipal workers, hiring freezes, and reductions in sanitation, libraries, and in other areas. Despite all these cuts, fire and police services, sanitation, welfare programs, public housing and education are more expensive than they need to be. The reason goes back to widespread individual irresponsibility which forces government to spend money. Self-control would eliminate the need for or cut many programs. Responsible behavior will result if we ask for it. Information is the key.

LEADERSHIP

The answer to the question of who will manage these information and persuasive communications programs is a coalition of public and private institutions. Government, religious, civic, corporate, and civil rights leaders must cooperate to make sure the job is done well and fairly. White corporate, religious, civic, and government managers have been scrutinized in depth in the last decade, and they seem prepared to cooperate in a sophisticated joint multidimensional crime prevention program.

For their part, black leaders have been ambivalent about crime. For them to contribute skills and credibility, they have to reach consensus on the importance of crime prevention in economic development. Those who engage in destructive behavior are more likely to respond to the exhortations of black leaders. Indeed, most information-communication-explanation-persuasion might best come from black leaders. This is not to say that poor and marginal African Americans will respond only to black messages. Perhaps in some circumstances, such messages might be coun-terproductive. Nonetheless, civil rights leaders can have a major impact.

Suppose we agree on a package of crime prevention strategies and on the critical importance of communication-persuasion-explanation to deterrence. Who should do the communicating—government, churches, corporate leaders, or civic leaders? The answer is all of them. Public and private institutions and leaders are responsible for sending out the word; civil rights leaders have a special role to play in the process.

Correcting destructive behavior is not easy for individuals, families, institutions, or nations. The have nots cannot reform themselves without help; for better or worse they have a stake in the status quo. Reform is not strictly government's responsibility; rather, a public-private partnership is required. The payoffs—prosperity, security, growth, freedom, and opportunity—will be shared broadly. Black leaders can play a dramatic role in reducing crime; they can work with all these tools, using both direct and indirect information devices, to change behavior. And they can support innovative and conventional law enforcement unequivocally.

10

The Social Debt and Tax Reform

Fellow citizens, we cannot escape history. . . . As our case is new, so
we must think anew, and act anew.

—Abraham Lincoln

You can always count on Americans to do the right thing, after they
have tried everything else.

—Winston Churchill

To create and sustain broad economic prosperity, we need, among other
things, a wise and balanced tax program. Throughout the 1970s and 1980s
taxes became a unique political tool in the hands of racial demagogues.
The "No New Taxes" pledge in 1988 was actually racial code language
meaning no taxes would be used for "social engineering." While it had
emotional and political appeal, it was a distorted policy. Fiscal discipline
is important, as is budget control. Moreover, waste is high and must be
reduced. What to do, however, means guessing at how voters will
respond to changes. And most politicians are averse to risk.

Changes in income taxes, capital gains, local property, and social
security taxes all produce mixed and often unpredictable incentives,
affecting productivity, creativity, and total output. However, we don't
really know what the investment or employment consequences will be.
Constant proposals are being made to adjust the tax strucutre—earned
income credits, children's exemptions, capital gains, and so on—whether
in contraction or expansion, ideological debate never ends.[1]

As with every other aspect of public policy, tax policy that will truly
benefit the haves and the middle and also lift the have nots is not feasible
without taking account of the social debt and the need for redistributive

restitution.[2] That idea has not come up anywhere in our discussion until now. Although taxes affect efficiency and resource allocation,[3] they also are intended to produce equity. They have a legitimate redistributive function and should compensate for inherent injustices in the workings of the market.[4] Thus, tax policy will not strengthen the economy to truly produce benefits for the middle classes until both they and the haves acknowledge that taxes should, in part, raise revenues to pay the social debt, through all the "social engineering" programs outlined earlier.

PROGRESSIVE TAXATION AND RESTITUTION

Paying the social debt requires tax reform, which here means progressive, effective taxes, even if the taxes are simplified and "flatter" than before. Such reform will generate revenues that will be redistributed from the haves to the have nots through education, housing and business investment, health, behavior modification, education, and employment. This investment will produce security, investment, creativity, productivity, and jobs.

Making restitution in this way is not a precise way to handle it. Although it is not a perfect solution, as Boris Bittker notes, we do not have to wait for perfect remedies before we remedy serious lingering maladies as best we can. Capital can be raised through taxes. To correct imbalances between the top 30 and bottom 30 percent and especially the top 20 and bottom 20 percent, we need to adjust taxes to take more from the top. This suggestion is not particularly radical. In any case, the tax system needs fixing, and this is just one more good reason to get on with it.

The reallocation must be made in a way that is accepted by the haves, for tax reforms that are confiscatory and unjust will be of little value. Taxes can act as disincentives, but in most debates, the only kind of disincentives discussed are those to investors. Taxes, coupled with the budgetary component of fiscal policy, can act as incentives or disincentives to wage and salary earners of all kinds.[5] The reforms, then, need broad concurrence, with everyone understanding the reasons for tax policy and ultimately viewing the tax structure as fair. Thus, full explanation and good information are crucial to success. Eventually, restitution has to make sense to at least 51 percent of the electorate and, better 66 to 75 percent. It needs bipartisan political support from people of goodwill who occupy the middle of the road politically.

TAX REFORM AND REDISTRIBUTION

Tax policy has a proper explicit redistributive and equity function and can create opportunity and incentives for the previously excluded. With gross national product of $5.6 trillion, $300 billion in federal tax revenues can be raised, but $250 billion is lost through loopholes. A simpler, fairer system would capture some of that amount. Then investment in housing, behavior, health, education, training, and business development for the bottom thirty would in time generate more tax revenues as they became more productive. In that way, paying the debt will spur general growth and benefit everyone.

SOAK THE RICH

In 1992 Robert S. McIntyre, director of Citizens for Tax Justice in Washington, wrote in *Challenge* magazine that tax "inequality" undermines economic performance.[6] That is quite an understatement. Increasing federal taxes by 30 percent on the top 1 percent would produce $84 billion in 1992, he estimated. Sixty thousand families have taxable incomes of over $1 million. In the 1980s, however, taxes on the rich were lowered.[7] If we simply restored the system to roughly the progressivity it had in 1978, that is, just adjust the then existing code for inflation, 75 percent of all families would have lower federal taxes and total tax revenues to the treasury would increase $76 billion annually, on average.

In 1989, 790,000 taxpayers, the top three-tenths of 1 percent, had adjusted gross incomes of $200,000.[8] That totaled $409 billion. They paid $96 billion in taxes at a 24.1 percent rate. Back in 1979, however, there were only 94,000 such people, and their effective marginal tax rate was 45.3 percent. Thus, the effective rate went down 20 percentage points for them, almost 50 percent. A surtax of, say, 20 percent on that income would produce $82 billion, unless the haves avoided the taxes in mass or the changes generated major backlash, acting as a disincentive, as supply side theorists would anticipate. A smaller surtax on those earning $100,000 to $200,000 would produce $100 billion. Beyond that, some people earn $1 million. What about their taxes?

WINNERS AND LOSERS

From 1979 to 1988, the top 10 percent's share of total wealth increased from 67.5 percent to 73.1 percent, and its share of after-tax income went up from 29.5 percent in 1980 to 34.9 percent in 1990.[9] Five percent of all families today earn over $100,000 and 1 percent earn over $200,000. The federal tax bill for the top 1 percent of families decreased 17.6 percent from 1977 to 1992, but those in the middle, and up to the top 20 percent, had tax increases.[10] The top 20 percent paid 69 percent of all federal taxes in 1992. That was up from 56 percent in 1980, because their incomes grew disproportionately. The top 5 percent comprises 3.3 million families. So. 13.2 million are in the top 20 percent and 19.8 million in the top 30 percent.

OTHER TAXES

Charles Walker and Martin Feldstein have proposed a consumption tax, or national sales tax, to replace the income tax. It might be simpler to administer, but it would probably introduce other distortions in investment and consumption. It would not lead to progressive changes in income distribution, and it would not help pay the social debt.

Tax reform means lower taxes for most people and, of course, higher taxes for others. Changing formulas for investment tax credits (ITCs) and the accelerated cost recovery system (ACRS) will also help the movement toward equity. These business incentives did not really attract investment to key productive sectors as had been touted. What they offered was simply shelter—avoidance. Billions of public revenues are lost in this way, since businesses invest in plants and equipment only when a market really exists. Firms have often been rewarded for doing what they would have done anyway. If we moderately decrease ITCs and ACRS, it won't hurt investment in plants and equipment. It will generate higher revenues and lead to greater fairness in income distribution after taxes.

The corporate tax rate was 46 percent; then it was cut to 34 percent. But deductions and credits still lower the effective rate dramatically for many firms. A trade union-funded study group, Citizens for Tax Justice, found that, of 250 profitable companies, 128 paid no federal taxes in a recent year, while earning $57 billion. Banks and insurance companies average 1.2 percent of pretax profits in income taxes, chemical firms, 7 percent, pharmaceuticals, 20 percent, and computer and office equipment companies, 26 percent.

In the mid-1980s a tax reform proposal would have increased corporate income taxes by $22 billion a year, or 25 percent. It would also have cut individual taxes by about the same amount. Many economists think such plans would improve overall economic efficiency, but what about equity? Does moving tax policy in that direction contribute to paying the social debt? Does it generate the broad benefits that can come from upgrading the have nots' skills and earning purchasing power?

Restitution theory adds a new dimension to our understanding of economic injustice, and it allows us to evaluate tax reform from this new perspective. Ronald Reagan said, ''The taxing power of the government must not be used to regulate the economy or bring about social change.'' However, that is precisely what taxes are for, in addition to raising revenue for basic government functions. So here is a stark confrontation between diametrically opposed public policy philosophies. Hopefully, restitution theory can moderate all views and lead to a constructive synthesis.

TAX FAIRNESS

Internal Revenue loses $95 billion a year on income earned underground but not reported. A fairer tax system, conscious that it is a redistributive tool, could pick up most of that revenue. That is because more people would tend to respect it and comply voluntarily. According to the polls, there is wide displeasure over the tax system. But Social Security payroll taxes fall heaviest on the bottom 30 percent. We need to adjust these taxes so that the poor can keep more of their earned income after taxes. Here's another way to slice it: the top 40 gets 70 percent of total earned income, and pays 25 percent in taxes, but the bottom 40 gets 15 percent of earned income and pays 22 percent in taxes. In 1980 a family of four at the then poverty line paid $462 in taxes; by 1984 this figure was up to $1,079. The disproportionate share of taxes paid by the have nots remains striking.

THE MEEK SHALL INHERIT?

Historical relationships reflect the general tax pattern through most of the post–World War II period. The haves, especially those in the top 10 percent, always find ways to escape their proportionate share, which helps explain the chronic revenue and deficit problems. It contributes to the sense of fundamental injustice felt by a broad cross-section of the American people. It also helps explain basic problems that undermine economic performance.

Whatever its flaws, the progressive system redistributes income, and to the extent that it does that fairly and well, it deserves to survive. If it should be replaced one day, then it should be superseded by a tax that is stepped so that high-income people pay a higher effective rate. We need a progressive system but one that is not too steep and has few shelters. In that way we will solve revenue and equity problems, and will retain incentives for capital and labor.

THE RIGHT DIRECTION

Senator Bill Bradley (D–N.J.) has called for a tax of 19 percent on single people making under $25,000 and on couples making over $40,000. The haves in the top 20 percent would pay a surtax on adjusted gross income. Sixty-five percent of all taxpayers would pay less; 20 percent would come out the same; and the top 15 would pay more because some important loopholes would be closed. That proportion seems about right. Something along those lines, a four-step tax was included in tax reform legislation in the late 1980s, but by the early 1990s it was clear that further reform was needed. It was also clear that public attitudes had not been prepared for the kind of fundamental reform needed to promote efficiency and equity. Too many voters were still being led to think simplistically about how to minimize taxes; they were not encouraged to reflect on the true full purpose of taxes.

NEGATIVE INCOME TAXES

The negative income tax is another proposal that would use the tax system to redistribute income. Since it would be in cash, not in-kind, it might be the most efficient way. Milton Friedman proposed the idea in the early 1960s, following which it has been advocated in some form by Presidents Nixon, Ford, and Carter. It can be justified, in part, as can any other redistributive tax reform, on the grounds that it will help pay the social debt. However, changing taxes will change not only the shares of income earned by class, but also how ethnic groups and regions make out.

There are also interregional discrepancies in shares of federal expenditures, with some states consistently paying more in taxes than they receive in federal outlays. Redistribution from the Frost to the Sun Belt tends to reinforce racial and class income disparities, because areas in the Sun Belt receiving funds disproportionately are affluent. In general, the Frost Belt sends money through Washington to the Sun Belt. The reason is political leverage, not rational resource allocation or equity. Groups interested in fair federal shares and economic revival have condemned the current situation.

HOW TO FUND RENEWAL

A number of proposals have been made to correct the ill effects of these disparities:

Reconstruction Finance Corporation. A national version of the New York Municipal Assistance Corporation. It would target industries and cities for investment, and in return, these industries would innovate and reform their operations and strategies.

National Economic Policy Board. Former Secretary of Labor Ray Marshall developed this idea. It would include business, labor, government, and other experts to help target public and private investment.

Industrial Development Bank. An idea that goes back to Senators Hubert Humphrey and Jacob Javits. Lester Thurow and Robert Reich have revived it to channel loans to new industries and to old ones trying to revitalize.

Regional Development Banks. To avoid Washington control, to put low-interest loans into promising industries and into cities' infrastructure and key services.

These would presumably change the bias in funding and give greater attention to the Frost Belt. They would also generate new business, products, and jobs, and streamline and modernize older, traditional industries.

VOTER AMBIVALENCE

Americans' attitudes toward public spending fluctuate. Proposition B, which limited California's budget in the late 1970s, reflected tight-fistedness, but by 1982 voters went for public improvements they would have defeated two years earlier. Throughout the 1980s and into the 1990s, voters and taxpayers sent mixed signals. The consistent element was their desire for quality public sector services and projects with no waste, but they also wanted to avoid income redistribution through fiscal policy. There's the rub.

The electorate votes to tax themselves or to approve bond issues for prisons, parks, housing, community development, roads, schools, hospitals, water treatment, sewers, and other public structures. It just depends on who benefits. Perhaps a careful explanation by the right leaders could help voters recognize the need to pay the social debt as well. Then everyone would agree to tax and spend for quality crime prevention and for social engineering investment.

Part of any campaign to prevent crime and reduce poverty is the need for better teachers in public schools. That means better teachers' colleges and higher salaries for good teachers. In 1991 votes in New Jersey rejected these educational improvements, perhaps because the issue had not been explained properly. They apparently failed to see the connection between their overall economic well-being and the investment required in the have nots.

TAX REFORM TO STIMULATE SMALL BUSINESS

Tax reform is needed to achieve equity and to pay the social debt. It is also needed to stimulate efficiency, creativity, risk taking, invention, innovation, productivity, savings, investment, and growth. Here tax reform means steeper effective income tax rates, fewer shelters and avoidances, less use of regressive sales and property taxes, and rates that enable the haves to contribute most in proportion to ability. It can also include reductions in targeted capital gains tax that can contribute directly to producing those desirable economic consequences.

The problem with capital gains tax cuts as a kind of "reform" is that they would not be targeted. Supply side tax reform, as intended by Arthur Laffer, KempRoth, and others, advocated the use of across-the-board cuts to stimulate aggregate output and savings and investment. Growth was presumed to follow, and the so-called rising tide would lift all boats. It never worked out that way in the 1980s.

The United States has one of the highest per capita incomes in the world but contributes less per capita in taxes than most industrialized Western nations. That is often what liberals are concerned about when they speak of tax reform. However, conservative opponents of that kind of reform often advocate simply lowering taxes, with broad positive effects benefiting have nots, haves, and those in the middle. Restitution theory will help clear up this muddle, but until explicit equity enters the debate, neither side can get it right.

Tax and municipal finance reform will remain stymied until restitution theory takes hold. Then we will be able to think clearly and act constructively on tax reform. The haves owe a social debt, and progressive taxation is a way—imperfect, to be sure—to pay it. But we also want to stimulate business, and that requires moderate corporate and capital gains taxes. As often happens, we have to balance competing legitimate policy objectives.

BUSINESS ATTITUDES

Many people believe that the public sector is inefficient, and some see income redistribution as an essential part of the solution to our problems. They understand that only government can redistribute income and wealth equitably. Although some political and business leaders also recognize that redistribution is needed to solve the economy's problems, they have not yet grasped restitution theory as part of the rationale. So there has been an unproductive, circular discussion that has led nowhere for twenty years. Restitution theory, of course, is not yet accepted by the Conference Board or the National Association of Manufacturers, the Business Roundtable, the U.S. Chamber of Commerce, the Public Affairs Council, or the Business-Government Relations Council. Businesspeople know that government is often inefficient and must be improved; at the same time, they want to keep government out of their affairs. Most of all, they want to avoid progressive tax reform and to lower taxes and gain greater incentives.

Government understands their wishes, but progressive tax reform is overdue. Somehow political and business leaders have to get together and explain why redistribution is needed if everyone is to enjoy security and growth. Some progressive business and political leaders see the need for higher effective corporate and personal taxes and are aware that more redistribution must take place. These farsighted leaders recognize the broad public interest but have not yet come up with a compelling argument that could convince a majority. So the economy suffers.

11

Security, Productivity, Competitiveness, Economic Strategy, and Restitution

Prosperity can only be lasting if it is based on justice.
—Theodore Roosevelt

During the 1980s politicians jockeyed for advantage by using alternative visions of economic renewal. Doom and gloom alternated with a mood of "It's Morning in America." Attempts were also made to fashion bipartisan long-range economic policies based on intelligent high-mindedness. During this period, the economy expanded. Equities boomed, certain kinds of service jobs were created, and a widely shared benefit appeared to come from a deficit-driven strategy focused heavily on public sector investment in defense. During this same period, however, the Catholic bishops offered a Pastoral Letter on the economy calling for modifying "dehumanizing tendencies within capitalism." It asked for a reexamination of national values to produce fairness and justice for poor people. The bishops had an intuitive grasp of restitution theory.

SOCIAL ENGINEERING

A constant flow of critiques urges a redirection of national strategies. In emphasizing pieces of the problem, their remedies are incomplete. Robert Kuttner's *The End of Laissez Faire*,[1] Robert Reich's *The Work of Nations*,[2] and Michael Porter's *The Competitive Advantage of Nations*,[3] represent three thoughtful examinations produced in the early 1990s. Also outspoken are the think tanks—the Brookings Institution, American Enterprise Institute, Cato Institute, Heritage Foundation, Hudson Institute, Urban Institute, Hoover Institution, Center for National Priorities, Progressive Policy Institute, Economic Policy Institute and the Joint Center for Political and Economic Studies, among ohers. Restitution theory did not factor in their analyses, however, and so their work led to incomplete recommendations and, ironically, contributed to the policy and performance shortfall. Restitution theory is a primary component of any attempt to attack the problem of overall economic performance.

THE ROAD TO RENEWAL

Let us summarize a few representative analyses and recommendations for economic renewal. In one form or another these have been debated since the end of the Vietnam War. Even so, we still have not arrived at a strategy that will promote international competitiveness and at the same time strengthen the basic domestic economy by investing adequately in all citizens.

William J. Abernathy, Kim B. Clark, and Alan M. Kantrow, in *Industrial Renaissance*,[4] showed how new technologies have transformed business and what the new environment will mean for traditional industries. Most of their research focused on the auto industry, whose problems, they argued, are typical of basic industry. They concluded that Americans have to strive for excellence in basic manufacturing. These authors, however, failed to take sufficient account of destructive behavior—the subtle erosion of productivity, loyalty, and teamwork caused by workers' feelings of repressed outrage against economic injustice. They also overlooked the impact of poor discipline on worker performance. These are common oversights in scholarly works today.

The Abernathy et al. work contains some sophisticated comments about people management and human resource management, but they would probably view concern for economic injustice as, in their words, "waving the bloody shirt of long-standing grievance," rather than as integral to an economic renaissance. They see our problem as basically stemming from a failure to change technology, develop new products, adjust management practices, and improve labor relations. Improving labor relations, however, requires, among other things, that we recognize the social debt. It also requires increased sharing of information between labor and management to change behavior.

Next, let us examine Paul R. Lawrence and Davis Dyer's work, *Renewing American Industry*,[5] which looks at the internal ability of organizations to adapt and cope. Like Abernathy, Clark, and Kantrow, Lawrence and Dyer believe that the key to restoring America's economic health lies primarily within the firm and in management improvements.

In *The Next American Frontier*,[6] Robert Reich states that we need to shift to new products and new markets to achieve economic revival. He says we need to get away from standard traditional high-volume production. He sees little hope for renewal of basic industry through the better management that Abernathy, Clark, Kantrow, Lawrence, and Dyer believe possible. Reich deplores "paper entrepreneuralism" and claims we have been hurt by myopic financial management. In addition, he notes that the United States is suffering from the boom in clever but shallow and shortsighted divestiture and acquisition strategies. As remedies, he proposes that government be given a primary role in the shift to high tech. Reich says that we need a comprehensive, activist, direct interventionist government that should design and implement industrial strategy along the lines of the Japanese and German models. According to Reich, deteriorating productivity is a principal problem. Consequently, he advocates the establishment of a central industrial review board that will help produce national industrial strategies; more federal funding of dislocated worker retraining; and changed antitrust and tax laws to facilitate joint research and discourage merger game playing.

The way we organize for work (and for politics) Reich states, has everything to do with how well we produce and prosper. Our competitive advantage in high-volume mass production has eroded since the mid-1960s, while other countries have accelerated into those markets. With our competitive advantages in knowledge and information activities and in precision-designed high-tech products and processes, investment in people, he believes, becomes the most important item. But we have underinvested.

Reich's recommendations differ from other economic prescriptions currently being touted. He explicitly recognizes that social justice is a precondition to further growth and development. He wants us to shift from basic steel to custom steel, from low-skilled car assembly and production of simple components to complex components, from cotton, wool, and simple synthetic textiles to carbon fibers, especially polyesters, and from simple machine tools to computer-assisted manufacturing. All these changes would require skilled labor, which means better on-the-job training. Advanced technologies would reduce labor costs and upgrade workers' abilities to solve problems and improve efficiency and quality.

Reich agrees that employees are often incompetent, tardy, absent, and careless and that such behavior reflects their alienation, helping to undermine overall economic performance. They perform this way, however, mainly because government scrimps on education, mass transit, public housing, day care, and health, in his view. Reich also notes that we hurt ourselves by hanging on to mythical notions, especially that of the self-made person under free enterprise. That insight suggests Reich's implicit understanding of how economic injustice destroys the United States' economic structure. What he calls "civic virtue"—that is, Behave Yourself—can be promoted by improved explanation and information. Ultimately, Reich is most interested in improving the United States' competitiveness, but the road to this goal, he says, is by increasing personal capability and skill rather than by merely tinkering with organizations, budgets, regulations, and fiscal and monetary policy. Improved competitiveness will take more than a combination of Abernathy et al.'s better management and Reich's call for civic virtue and greater investment in human capital. As a precondition, these all require recognizing and curing economic injustice and stopping or dissuading destructive behavior.

Reich wants the government to grant tax incentives to hurting industries in order to help them invest more in worker training and education and in new technologies. He would set up regional development banks to help finance these lame industries to recovery. He also advocates "industrial policy." The United States has lost ground in international markets; the nation is plagued by chronic trade deficits and is vulnerable in strategically important research and science-based industries—all of which makes us nervous. Industrial policy would, first, target government spending, taxing, and regulations to help selected industries or regions that are considered strategically important or have potentially high growth. Second, it would help ease adjustment to leaner revenues and smaller markets for declining industries.

Industrial policy need not involve much central planning or protectionism. It is basically government working with business, labor, and academia to smooth market shocks and hasten the development of neglected or impeded activities or products thought to be worthwhile. The trouble with industrial policy is that it fails to recognize destructive behavior—crime and injustice—as central problems. From the point of view of many conservative observers, like Senator Philip Gramm, Representative Newt Gingrich, Jack Kemp, and writers like Irving Kristol, Kevin Phillips, Evans and Novak, of course, it has other serious defects. They would prefer drastic deregulation and tax cuts, and they would expect laissez-faire results to be broadly positive.

The interventionist approach calls for federal investment banks, advanced technology centers, public/private committees on industry targeting, state development banks, new training programs, and export promotion, all of which are good techniques if they are managed properly. Conceptually, however, that package is also inadequate. It misses a prime ingredient, just as does naive total reliance on free market resource allocation. We have to recognize and correct the social debt.

Managements have failed to maintain morale and to offer dignified incentives to workers. The result has been quality and productivity decline, as Abernathy, Clark, and Kantrow correctly note, and as Thomas J. Peters and Robert H. Waterman show in *In Search of Excellence*. Labor and management don't have to cohabit, but there's a corrosive sense of historic economic injustice that is broadly felt. It contributes to the attitudes that lead to chronic labor-management antagonism and to other detrimental consequences.

Abernathy et al. believe that international markets (e.g., in autos) gave clear enough signals to American managers to stimulate change, but they were slow in reading these signals and responding. Reich does not believe that the markets work very well. Abernathy et al. think that improvements in labor-management relations can have a major effect on manufacturing quality but that is not likely unless an attempt is made to redress the inherent wrongs in income and wealth distribution that workers sense and to deal with the resulting destructive attitudes and behaviors.

A fourth view is espoused by Samuel Bowles, David M. Gordon, and Thomas E. Weisskopf's in *After the Wasteland: A Democratic Economics for the Year 2000*.[7] They see cumulative deterioration in output, productivity, and employment, and as a reason why they believe that the system is wasteful, irrational, top heavy and overly preoccupied with profit. They point specifically to economic ills, such as unemployment, idle factories, superfluous supervisors and midlevel administrators, failure to innovate, inefficient health care, and a wasteful military. As solutions, they propose making better use of labor, knowledge, and raw materials, avoiding hypersocial competition by raising minimum wages, adopting equal pay for equal worth, redistributing rewards more equally and fairly, organizing work to encourage participation, producing essential goods and services and less "junk," and conserving the environment.

The Bowles work is among the few that sees a clear connection between chronic inequity and general decline. But they err in the other direction. They too heavily discount the market's incentives to creativity and problem solving. They want "economic democracy," by which they mean variations on traditional investor ownership and control, involving other stakeholders—workers, customers, and the community.

Lester Thurow, in the *Zero Sum Society*,[8] claims that we are stuck because none of our problems can be solved without making some group worse off. However, our political system allows for, and perhaps even encourages, stalemate, and groups can nullify policies that threaten them even if the whole society might benefit. Thurow also clearly sees that income and wealth redistribution is involved in any policy that can produce success. Facing up to that realization is paramount, and getting political concurrence is tricky. Leaders must explain who must bear the costs and then win adherence, but politicians generally don't like to talk about income redistribution.

Thurow worries that our system does not allocate losses well. Accordingly, he wants government to face equity questions and help citizens understand them and respond intelligently. Specifically, he advocates massive public investments, especially in energy alternatives and in industries with high growth potential; greater savings stimulated by budget deficits and tax cuts for the middle classes; guaranteed jobs and increased opportunities in occupations previously restricted by race and gender; and support for any groups hurt by public policy that seeks to accelerate strategic development in certain sectors at the expense of others. Thurow correctly recognizes that economic growth cannot solve the problem because poor people want justice, that is, parity, not simply more. But "where should parity demands be met and where should parity demands be rejected? What principles should underlay this acceptance or rejection?" The answer is restitution theory; social accounting will help us make better policy.

Theodore Sorensen, one of President Kennedy's most valued advisers, called for bipartisan cooperation in his book *A Different Kind of Presidency*.[9] He gave us only until 1990 to begin to seriously cooperate; after that, he thought, irreparable damage would have been done to our industrial base, infrastructure, human capital stock, and international relations. Let us hope we have more time. Specifically, Sorensen claims that our manufacturing sector has slipped absolutely and that relatively unstable conditions, politically based trade, tax and regulatory, and monetary policies are hurting us. As remedies, he proposed holding down interest rates, adopting trade policies that will help increase foreign markets, finding ways to ensure stable growth, protecting the dollar but not unbalancing its strength, and supporting basic research.

Some of these observers—for example, Thurow, Bowles, Gordon, and Weisskopf—point to the United States' poor macroeconomic, fiscal, and monetary policy. Reich cites inconsistent government policy. Looking at Japan's example, he concludes that American managers have overemphasized short-term financial management and control and structural manipulation, and need to look to the long term. Still others—Lawrence and Dye, Peters and Waterman, as well as Abernathy, Clark, and Kantrow—look at management and see opportunities to roll up our sleeves and do better at organization and leadership, raising productivity and morale. Many other observers and advocates, left, right, and center, also have valuable insights and analyses to share, but curing economic injustice is missing from most of them. Adding this insight yields a comprehensive program.

Finally, Paul Hawken's *The Next Economy*,[10] has a different outlook from any of the works mentioned in this chapter. He thinks we are in a major transition. To him, and others like him, renewal, renaissance, and abetting decline are inadequate objectives. The simple fact, he says, is that we are leaving the industrial age, and nothing we can do about public policy or improved management can do much to change this basic truth. We have entered the information economy and so it is that we will need fewer resources and more and better information. Accordingly, we need to design and produce more intelligently and to substitute knowledge for material. Basically, we are already doing this because energy is getting too expensive.

Hawken does not think our economy is ill; it is merely changing, he says. He also thinks that in the twenty-first century Americans will be personally and collectively less aggressive, competitive, and harsh. In a sense, he anticipates more attitudes of Behave Yourself throughout society. His prediction is that we will use less, have more, and behave more wisely. He feels it is pointless to argue about the present economic structure's defects when it is actually being discarded. That may overstate the matter. Indeed, our industries will continue to be based on raw material and to be central to our economy, although the changing ratio of material to information in all products, as he notes, will increasingly favor information.

TO RESTORE THE SOCIAL FABRIC

The economy of the twenty-first century will be based on highly sophisticated, creative new products and services. The businesses thus produced will be highly entrepreneurial. Government can encourage their creativity and growth, but it should basically give them room and not try to plan and guide that process too closely. Government's main role is to see to it that social equity is realized and that little or no social exploitation takes place in the course of our twenty-first–century economic propulsion. Preventing exploitation and its damaging consequences for labor and capital incentives is a high priority. Coercive illegitimate diversions of income should be spotted and monitored through improved national income accounts, and attention should be focused on the measurable consequences of economic injustice. This approach in itself will be remedial. Then we can retrieve and redistribute (democratically through tax and budgetary processes) such wrongfully exploited benefits from unjust economic relationships. Otherwise, we need to let business do business.

LET THE GOOD TIMES ROLL

The road to prosperity is filled with social debt potholes produced by economic injustice throughout our history. If we are going to fix our infrastructure and restore our country's vitality, we will have to pay the debts. Our goals are to raise living standards, end our industrial decline, generate jobs, create an environment for successful investment and creativity, strengthen our manufacturing base, and move to the next economy. Many prescriptions are available, and they will all get a hearing. Surely, however, we will not prosper unless we end our destructive behavior, make restitution, and restore the social compact of acceptable behavior. In the next twenty years, we can use new information and new information technologies to solve two of the chronic ills that have threatened us with loss and decay. By succeeding in that endeavor, we will help bolster our freedoms and protect our paychecks and homes and savings. We can restore the social fabric, and let the good times roll, but only with justice for all.

Notes

INTRODUCTION

1. Spencer Rich, "Food Stamps Now a Fact of Life for 25 Million in U.S.," *Washington Post*, May 23, 1992, p. 1.

2. Boris Bittker, *The Case for Black Reparations* (Random House, 1972).

3. See, for example, "The Economic Crisis of Urban America," *Business Week*, May 18, 1992.

4. A useful summary of economic research on slavery and its role in development is in Richard F. America, ed., *The Wealth of Races: The Present Value of the Benefits from Past Injustices* (Greenwood Press, 1990).

5. Lawrence Kotlikoff, *Generational Accounting* (Macmillan, 1991).

6. See Herbert Inhaber and Sidney Carroll, *How Rich Is Too Rich? Income and Wealth in America* (Praeger, 1992).

CHAPTER 1

1. "Study Calls U.S. a Country Deeper in Debt to Minorities," *New York Times*, May 24, 1988.

2. Andrew Brimmer, "Blacks Make Moderate Gains in Labor Market," *Black Enterprise*, April 1986.

3. In Frank McCoy, "Achieving Growth in a Slowly Reviving Economy," *Black Enterprise*, January 1992, p. 51.

4. See David Swinton, "Racial Inequality and Reparations," in *The Wealth of Races: The Present Value of the Benefits from Past Injustices*, ed. Richard F. America (Greenwood Press, 1990), p. 153

5. "The Economy: A Gloomy Forecast," *Focus*, The Magazine of the Joint Center for Political Studies, February–March 1992, p. 9.

6. David Wessel, "Money Talks, the Wealthy Watch Gains of 1980s Become Political Liabilities," *Wall Street Journal*, April 8, 1992.

7. Robert J. Samuelson, "The Fictitious Issue of the 'Jobs Gap'—and the Damage It Can Cause," *Washington Post*, September 14, 1988.

8. Andrew F. Brimmer, "Building Wealth and Assets," *Black Enterprise*, July 1991, p. 31.

9. Richard D. Hylton, "Confronting the Challenges of a Changing Economy," *Black Enterprise*, January 1988.

10. Gary S. Becker, "Why a Depression Isn't in the Cards," *Business Week*, November 9, 1987.

11. See Larry Neal, "A Calculation and Comparison of the Current Benefits of Slavery and an Analysis of Who Benefits," in *The Wealth of Races: The Present Value of the Benefits from Past Injustices*, ed. Richard F. America (Greenwood Press, 1990), p. 91, and James Marketti, "Estimated Present Value of Income Diverted During Slavery," in ibid., p. 107.

12. Lester Thurow, *Poverty and Discrimination* (Brookings Institution, 1969), p. 12.

13. Berkeley Working Paper #1, "An Illustrative Estimate: The Present Value of the Benefits from Racial Discrimination, 1929-1969," in *The Wealth of Races: The Present Value of the Benefits from Past Injustices*, ed. Richard F. America (Greenwood Press, 1990), pp. 163-68.

14. Lester Thurow, *Generating Inequality* (Basic Books, 1975).

15. See Berkeley Working Paper #1.

16. Daniel P. Moynihan, *Maximum Feasible Misunderstanding* (Free Press, 1970).

17. Thomas B. Edsall, "Bush's Blue-Collar Problem," *Washington Post*, July 3, 1988.

18. Sylvia Nasar, "Those Born Wealthy or Poor Usually Stay So, Studies Say," *New York Times*, May 19, 1992, p. 1.

19. John M. Berry, "U.S. Wealth Becomes More Concentrated," *Washington Post*, July 26, 1986.

20. Richard Bernstein, "20 Years after the Kerner Report," *New York Times*, February 29, 1988.

CHAPTER 2

1. Jean François Revel, *How Democracies Perish* (Harper and Row, 1985).

2. Ulrich B. Phillips, *American Negro Slavery* (D. Appleton, 1918) and *Life and Labor in the Old South* (Little, Brown, 1929).

3. Alfred Conrad and John Meyer, *The Economics of Slavery and Other Studies in Econometric History* (Aldine, 1964).

4. Roger L. Ransom and Richard Sutch, *One Kind of Freedom: The Economic Consequences of Emancipation* (Cambridge University Press, 1977).

5. Robert W. Fogel and Stanley L. Engerman, *Time on the Cross: The Economics of American Negro Slavery* (Little, Brown, 1974).

6. E. J. Dionne, Jr., "A Conservative Call for Compassion," *New York Times*, November 30, 1987.

7. Robert Nozick, "Distributive Justice," *Philosophy and Public Affairs* (Fall 1973): 45-126.

8. George Gilder, *Wealth and Poverty* (Basic Books, 1981).

9. Charles Murray, *Losing Ground: American Social Policy 1950-1980* (Basic Books, 1984).

10. Irving Kristol, "The Negro Today Is Like the Immigrant Yesterday," *New York Times*, September 11, 1966.

11. Theodore Hershberg, ed., *Philadelphia: Work, Space, Family and Group Experience in the 19th Century* (Oxford University Press, 1981).

12. Charles C. Krauthammer, "Reparations for Black Americans," *Time*, December 31, 1990.

13. Nathan Glazer, "Ethnicity and the Schools," *Commentary*, September 1974, p. 57.

14. Donald L. Horowitz, in a review of Glazer's *Affirmative Discrimination*, *Washington Post*, 1976.

15. Robert Nozick, interview in *Forbes*, March 15, 1975.

16. Boris Bittker, *The Case for Black Reparations* (Random House, 1972).

17. Hershberg, *Philadelphia*.

CHAPTER 3

1. William Bennett, *The Devaluing of America* (Summit, 1992).

2. Lester Thurow, *The Zero Sum Society: Distribution and the Possibilities for Economic Change* (Basic Books, 1980).

CHAPTER 5

1. Fact Sheet on Economic Policy, Joint Center for Political and Economic Studies (JCPES), January 23, 1992.

2. Ibid.

3. Black and White Households by Net Worth, 1988, Bureau of the Census, Current Population Reports, p. 70, No. 22. Tables 2 and 5.

4. Robert Reich, *The Work of Nations* (Alfred A. Knopf, 1991).

CHAPTER 6

1. William Julius Wilson, *The Truly Disadvantaged* (University of Chicago Press, 1988).

2. Michael B. Katz, *The Undeserving Poor: From the War on Poverty to the War on Welfare* (Pantheon, 1989).

3. Shelby Steele, *The Content of Our Character, A New Vision of Race in America* (HarperCollins, 1991).

4. Stephen L. Carter, *Confessions of an Affirmative Action Baby* (Basic Books, 1991).

5. Nathan Glazer, *Affirmative Discrimination* (Basic Books, 1986).

6. The White House, Office of National Services, "A Thousand Points of Light: The Third Hundred," 1991.

7. Amitai Etzioni, *A Responsive Society: Collected Essays on Guiding Deliberate Social Change* (Jossey-Bass, 1991).

8. James Reston, *San Francisco Chronicle*, April 25, 1971.

9. John Lindsay, *New York Times*, June 9, 1971. Emphasis added.

10. Richard Herrnstein, "I.Q.," *Atlantic*, September 1971.

11. William Raspberry, "The Value of Black Colleges," *Washington Post*, July 5, 1992.

12. Nathan Glazer, *San Francisco Chronicle*, Spring 1972.

13. Paul Seabury, "Burying the Hatchet," *Commentary*, April 1975.

CHAPTER 7

1. Sharon LaFraniere, "U.S. Has Most Prisoners Per Capita in the World," *Washington Post*, December 1991.

2. Howard Goodman, "U.S. Prison System Is a Modern Version of the Old Poorhouse," *Philadelphia Inquirer*, November 11, 1990.

3. Samuel L. Myers, Jr., "Crime Reporting and the True Crime Rate," *Social Science Quarterly* 61, No. 1 (June 1980): 23–45.

4. James Q. Wilson, *Thinking about Crime* (Basic Books, 1975).

5. Daniel Seligman, "The Coming Decline of Crime, review of James Q. Wilson's *Crime and Public Policy*," *Fortune*, August 22, 1983, p. 221.

6. See, for example, A.P., "U.S. Crime Rose 9 Percent in 1980: 23,044 Murdered," *Washington Post*, September 11, 1981.

7. Gloria Campisi, "The Elderly and Crime: A Study in Fear," *Philadelphia Daily News*, February 20, 1980.

8. Charles R. Babcock, "Panel Calls for Spending $2 Billion to Lock Up More Violent Criminals," *Washington Post*, August 18, 1981.

9. John Woestendieck, "In Pa. Prisons, Five Years Might Not Mean Five Years," *Philadelphia Inquirer*, November 21, 1982.

10. Stanton Samenow, *Inside the Criminal Mind* (Random House, 1984).

11. Terence Samuel, "Young Urban Blacks: A Study in Alienation," *Philadelphia Inquirer*, May 28, 1992.

12. Mary Walton, "'Wolfpacks': A New Kind of Gang Preys on City," *Philadelphia Inquirer*, November 23, 1980.

13. Joseph Volz, "Baltimore Study Finds Much Crime by Heroin Users," *Washington Post*, May 12, 1984.

14. Adrienne Washington, "Drug Link to Crime Disputed," *Washington Star*, November 3, 1980.

15. Christopher McCabe, "More Facts Given on Blacks in Prison," *Philadelphia Inquirer*, June 23, 1992.

16. William Raspberry, "Bringing Up Criminals," *Washington Post*, April 22, 1992.

CHAPTER 8

1. Thomas Lickoma, *Educating for Character: How Our Schools Can Teach Respect and Responsibility* (Bantam, 1991).

2. David O'Reilly, "An Initiative from Educators: Bring Back Values to the Class," *Philadelphia Inquirer*, November 17, 1991.

3. Courtland Milloy, "The Painful Games That Boys Play," *Washington Post*, April 30, 1991.

4. L. Douglas Wilder, "To Save the Black Family, the Young Must Abstain," *Wall Street Journal*, March 28, 1991.

5. Charles Murray, *Losing Ground: American Social Policy, 1950–1980* (Basic Books, 1986).

CHAPTER 9

1. Kim Foltz, "New Strategies Being Tried Against Drunk Driving," *New York Times*.

2. Stuart Elliott, Public Service Campaigns Ran at Record Pace in '90," *New York Times*, August 12, 1991.

3. Joanne Lipman, "Public Service Campaigns Benefit from Industry's Continued Slump," *Wall Street Journal*, November 6, 1991.

4. Stephen Knack, "Why We Don't Vote—Or Say "Thank You,'" *Wall Street Journal*, December 31, 1990.

5. William E. Schmidt, "They're Trying to Stop People from Being Beastly," *New York Times*, September 21, 1991.

6. Ronald Berman, *Advertising and Social Change* (Sage, 1981).

7. Seymour Fine, *The Marketing of Ideas and Social Issues* (Greenwood Press, 1981).

8. Philip Kotler, *Marketing for Nonprofit Organizations* (VTNC, Arlington, 1975).

9. James Q. Wilson, *Thinking About Crime*, rev. ed. (Basic Books, 1983).

10. Theodore Levitt, *The Marketing Imagination* (Free Press, 1986).

11. Leslie Berger, "National Crime and Violence Test," *Washington Post*, March 20, 1982, p. C10.

12. Howard Rosenberg, "After You See a Crime Re-enacted, They Flash a 'Wanted' Poster," *Philadelphia Inquirer*.

13. Leslie Bennetts, "Celebrities Join Mayor in New Battle Against Graffiti Writers," *New York Times*, April 30, 1982.

14. Stephanie Mansfield, "Littering 'Antisocial,' Target of Ads," *Washington Post*.

CHAPTER 10

1. Liberal and conservative views are fairly represented in Lester Thurow, *Head to Head* (Morrow, 1992) and Robert L. Bartley, *The Seven Fat Years* (Free Press, 1992).

2. The argument against redistribution is fairly summarized in Gordon Tullock, *Economics of Income Redistribution* (Kluwer-Nijhoff, 1983).

3. Michael Kinsley, "Brain Dead Tax Plan," *Washington Post*, March 26, 1992.

4. Even conservative economists are explicitly acknowledging that on occasion; see Herbert Stein, "Reflections on the Top 1%," *Wall Street Journal*, May 26, 1992.

5. John Liscio, "Uncle Sam as Robin Hood," *U.S. News & World Report*, June 1, 1992, p. 53.

6. William Raspberry, "The Blind Men and the Tax Code," *Washington Post*, 1992.

7. The frequent complaint that tax reforms in the 1980s unfairly benefited the top 1 percent is rebutted in Anne B. Fisher, "The New Debate over the Very Rich," *Fortune*, June 29, 1992.

8. Victor Perlo, "Who the Rich Are and What They Should Pay," *New York Times*, December 1, 1991.

9. E. J. Dionne, "Loss of Faith in Egalitarianism Begins to Reshape U.S. Social Policy," *Washington Post*, April 30, 1990.

10. R. A. Zaldivar, "Defining Who Is Wealthy," *Philadelphia Inquirer*, February 1992.

CHAPTER 11

1. Robert Kuttner, *The End of Laissez Faire: American Economic Policy after the Cold War* (Random House, 1991).

2. Robert Reich, *The Work of Nations: Preparing Ourselves for 21st Century Capitalism* (Alfred A. Knopf, 1991).

3. Michael Porter, *The Competitive Advantage of Nations* (Free Press, 1990).

4. William J. Abernathy, Kim B. Clark, and Alan M. Kantrow, *Industrial Renaissance: Producing a Competitive Future for America* (Basic Books, 1983).

5. Paul Lawrence and Davis Dyer, *Renewing American Industry* (Free Press, 1983).

6. Robert Reich, *The Next American Frontier* (Times Books, 1983).

7. Samuel Bowles, David M. Gordon, and Thomas E. Weisskopf, *After the Wasteland: A Democratic Economics for the Year 2000* (M. E. Sharpe, 1990).

8. Lester Thurow, *The Zero Sum Society: Distribution and the Possibilities for Economic Change* (Basic Books, 1980).

9. Theodore Sorensen, *A Different Kind of Presidency: A Proposal for Breaking the Political Deadlock* (Harper and Row, 1984).

10. Paul Hawken, *The Next Economy* (Ballantine, 1984).

Selected Bibliography

Abernathy, William J., Kim B. Clark, and Alan M. Kantrow. *Industrial Renaissance: Producing a Competitive Future for America*. Basic Books, 1983.

America, Richard F. *Developing the Afro-American Economy*. Lexington, Mass., 1977.

——— . ed. *The Wealth of Races: The Present Value of Benefits from Past Injustices*. Greenwood Press, 1990.

Ashenfelter, Orley and Albert Rees, eds. *Discrimination in Labor Markets*. Princeton University Press, 1974.

Auletta, Ken. *The Underclass*. Vintage, 1983.

Becker, Gary S. *The Economics of Discrimination*. University of Chicago Press, 1971.

Berman, Ronald. *Advertising and Social Change*. Sage, 1981.

Bittker, Boris. *The Case for Black Reparations*. Random House, 1972.

Boston, Thomas D. *Race, Class and Conservatism*. Unwin Hyman, 1988.

Bowles, Samuel, David M. Gordon, and Thomas E. Weisskopf. *After the Wasteland: A Democratic Economics for the Year 2000*. M. E. Sharpe, 1990.

Curtin, Philip D. *Atlantic Slave Trade: A Census*. University of Wisconsin Press, 1972.

Edwards, John. *Positive Discrimination and Social Justice*. Routledge, Chapman and Hall, 1987.

Eltis, David. *Economic Growth and the Ending of the Transatlantic Slave Trade*. Oxford University Press, 1987.

Fine, Seymour. *The Marketing of Ideas and Social Issues*. Greenwood Press, 1981.

Fleming, John E., Gerald R. Gill, and David H. Swinton. *The Case for Affirmative Action for Blacks in Higher Education*. Howard University Press, 1978.

Fogel, Robert W. and Stanley L. Engerman. *Time on the Cross: The Economics of American Negro Slavery*. Little, Brown, 1974.

Foner, Philip S. *The Black Worker: The Era of Postwar Prosperity and the Great Depression, 1920–1936*. Temple University Press, 1981.

Galbraith, John Kenneth. *The Nature of Mass Poverty*. Harvard University Press, 1979.

Garfinkel, Irwin and Robert H. Haveman. *Earnings Capacity, Poverty and Inequality*. Academic Press, 1977.

Gilder, George. *Wealth and Poverty*. Baisc Books, 1981.

Goldin, Claudia. *Urban Slavery in the American South*. University of Chicago Press, 1976.

Goldman, Alan H. *Justice and Reverse Discrimination*. Princeton University Press, 1979.

Gross, Barry R., ed. *Reverse Discrimination*. Prometheus Books, 1977.

Harrington, Michael. *The Other America*. Viking Penguin, 1971.

Harris, Fred and Roger Wilkins, eds. *Quiet Riots: Race and Poverty in the United States*. Pantheon, 1988.

Haveman, Robert H. *Poverty Policy and Poverty Research: The Great Society and the Social Sciences*. University of Wisconsin Press, 1987.

Hawken, Paul. *The Next Economy*. Ballantine, 1984.

Inhaber, Herbert and Sidney Carroll. *How Rich Is Too Rich? Income and Wealth in America*. Praeger, 1992.

Inikori, Joseph, ed. *Forced Migration: The Impact of the Export Slave Trade on African Societies*. Africana Publishing Co.

Katz, Michael B. *The Undeserving Poor: From the War on Poverty to the War on Welfare*. Pantheon, 1989.

Kotler, Philip. *Marketing for Nonprofit Organizations*. VTNC, Arlington, 1975.

Kotlikoff, Lawrence. *Generational Accounting*. Macmillan, 1991.

Kotlowitz, Alex. *There Are No Children Here*. Doubleday, 1991.

Kuttner, Robert. *The End of Laissez Faire: American Economic Policy after the Cold War*. Random House, 1991.

Lawrence, Paul R. and Davis Dyer. *Renewing American Industry*. Free Press, 1983.

LeGrand, Julian and Ray Robinson. *The Economics of Social Problems*. Harcourt Brace Jovanovich, 1980.

Levitt, Theodore. *The Marketing Imagination*. Free Press, 1986.

Levre, Ralph. *Cheap Labour and Racial Discrimination*. Gower Publishing Co., 1984.

Lipton, Michael. *Why Poor People Stay Poor: Urban Bias in World Development*. Harvard University Press, 1977.

Miller, David. *Social Justice*. Oxford University Press, 1976.

Miller, S. M. and Pamela Roby. *The Future of Inequality*. Basic Books, 1970.

Moynihan, Daniel P. *Family and Nation*. Harcourt Brace Jovanovich, 1986.

——— , ed. *On Understanding Poverty*. Basic Books, 1969.

Murray, Charles. *Losing Ground: American Social Policy, 1950–1980*. Basic Books, 1986.

Nash, Gary B. *Race and Revolution*. Madison House, 1990.

Nelson, John I. *Economic Inequality: Conflict Without Change*. Columbia University Press, 1982.

Oakes, Jeannie. *Keeping Track: How Schools Structure Inequality*. Yale University Press, 1986.

Peters, Thomas J. and Robert H. Waterman. *In Search of Excellence*. Harper & Row, 1982.

Phillips, Kevin. *The Politics of Rich and Poor*. Random House, 1990.

Phillips, Ulrich B. *American Negro Slavery: A Survey of the Supply, Employment, and Control of Negro Labor As Determined by the Plantation Regime*. Louisiana State University Press, 1966.

Porter, Michael. *The Competitive Advantage of Nations*. Free Press, 1990.

Ransom, Roger L. *Conflict and Compromise: The Political Economy of Slavery, Emancipation and the American Civil War*. Cambridge University Press, 1989.

—— and Richard Sutch. *One Kind of Freedom: The Economic Consequences of Emancipation*. Cambridge University Press, 1977.

Reich, Michael. *Racial Inequality: A Political-Economic Analysis*. Princeton University Press, 1981.

Reich, Robert. *The Next American Frontier*. Times Books, 1983.

—— . *The Work of Nations: Preparing Ourselves for 21st Century Capitalism*. Alfred A. Knopf, 1991.

Rodgers, Harrell R., Jr. *Poverty Amid Plenty: A Political and Economic Analysis*. Random House, 1979.

Schiller, Bradley R. *The Economics of Poverty and Discrimination*. Prentice-Hall, 1989.

Schorr, Lisbeth B. and Daniel Schorr. *Within Our Reach: Breaking the Cycle of Disadvantage and Despair*. Doubleday, 1988.

Sedlacek, William E. and Glenwood C. Brooks. *Racism in American Education: A Model for Change*. 1976.

Solow, Barbara L. *Slavery and the Rise of the Atlantic System*. Cambridge University Press, 1991.

Sorensen, Theodore. *A Different Kind of Presidency: A Proposal for Breaking the Political Deadlock*. Harper and Row, 1984.

Sowell, Thomas. *Race and Economics*. McKay, 1975.

—— . *Markets and Minorities*. Basic Books, 1981.

Thurow, Lester C. *Poverty and Discrimination*. Brookings Institution, 1969.

—— . *The Zero Sum Society: Distribution and the Possibilities for Economic Change*. Basic Books, 1980.

Wade, Richard C. *Slavery in the Cities: The South, 1820 to 1860*. Oxford University Press, 1965.

Walzer, Michael. *Spheres of Justice: A Defense of Pluralism and Equality*. Basic Books, 1983.

Williamson, Jeffrey G. and Peter H. Lindert. *American Inequality: A Microeconomic History*. Academic Press, 1980.

Wilson, James Q. *Thinking about Crime*. Basic Books, 1975.

Wilson, William Julius. *The Truly Disadvantaged*. University of Chicago Press, 1988.

Wise, Arthur E. *Rich Schools, Poor Schools: The Promise of Equal Educational Opportunity*. University of Chicago Press, 1972.

Index

About the Author

Richard F. America works in Washington, D.C., and is a Senior Program Manager in the federal government. He is the author of *Developing the Afro-American Economy* (1977), coauthor (with Bernard E. Anderson) of *Moving Ahead: Black Managers in American Business* (1978), and editor of *The Wealth of Races* (Greenwood Press, 1990). He was a Lecturer at the Schools of Business, University of California, Berkeley; Visiting Lecturer, Stanford Business School; and a Development Economist at Stanford Research Institute.